THE BUDDHIST CONCEPTION OF SPIRITS

THE BUDDHIST CONCEPTION OF SPIRITS

BIMALA CHURN LAW

SECOND EDITION
REVISED AND ENLARGED

GYAN

Published by

GYAN

Gyan Publishing House
5, Ansari Road
Daryaganj, New Delhi-110002
Phone: 011-47034999, 9811692060
E-mail: books@gyanbooks.com

Distribution Network
gyanbooks.com
India, USA, Canada, UK, Australia, France

ISBN : 978-81-212-3181-7 (PB)
First Published, London, 1936

2nd Impression 2020

Printed at: Gyan Press, Delhi.

The Buddhist Conception of Spirits
Author: B. C. Law

Law's Research Series, Pub. No. 3

THE BUDDHIST CONCEPTION OF SPIRITS

By

BIMALA CHURN LAW,

M.A., B.L., Ph.D.

Sir Asutosh Mookerjee Gold Medalist, Griffith Prizeman, Calcutta University; Honorary Correspondent, Archæological Survey of India; Advocate, High Court, Calcutta; Author: "A History of Pāli Literature," "Śrāvastī in Indian Literature," "Geography of Early Buddhism," "A Study of the Mahāvastu," "Some Kṣatriya Tribes of Ancient India," "Ancient Mid-Indian Kṣatriya Tribes," "Ancient Indian Tribes," "The Life and Work of Buddhaghosa," "Heaven and Hell in Buddhist Perspective," etc., etc.; Editor, "Buddhistic Studies"; Joint-Editor, "Indian Culture" and "Annual Bibliography of Indian Archæology" of the Kern Institute, Holland.

SECOND EDITION

REVISED AND ENLARGED

LUZAC & CO.

46, GREAT RUSSELL STREET, LONDON, W.C.1

1936

PREFACE TO THE FIRST EDITION

MY object, in writing this short treatise, has been to acquaint the public, as far as possible, with what the ancient Buddhists thought about spirits and spirit world. A study of the *Preta* belief among the Southern Buddhists is likely to be attractive. Materials have been drawn for the first time from the *Hīnayāna* Buddhist literature and specially from the *Paramatthadīpanī* (*The Elucidation of the Highest Meaning*) on the *Petavatthu* (*Preta* stories), that is the commentary on the *Petavatthu* which is one of the books of the *Khuddaka Nikāya*, written by Dhammapāla of Kāñcipura (Conjevaram). I fully agree with Mrs. Rhys Davids that the foolish little poems contained in the *Petavatthu* are no good but the stories given in its commentary present before us a very interesting side of the *Preta* belief. I am glad to find that the *Petavatthu* has been translated into German by Dr. Stede, but its commentary has not yet been translated into any modern language.

Professor Nilmani Chakravartty, M.A., has contributed a paper on "Spirit belief in the *Jātaka* Stories" (*JASB.*, x, New Series No. 7, 257–263) in which an attempt has been made to give a brief account of spirit belief, as far as it can be gathered from the *Jātaka* stories. The materials for his subject have been collected from the

Jātakas only save and except a very few which are noticed in my treatise.

I am indebted to Rao Saheb Dr. S. Krishnaswami Aiyangar, M.A., Ph.D., of the University of Madras, for his foreword.

BIMALA CHURN LAW.

24 SUKEA'S STREET,
CALCUTTA.
June, 1923.

PREFACE TO THE SECOND EDITION

THE first edition of this short treatise, published in 1923, has completely gone out of stock. That the first edition has been exhausted so soon from the date of its publication should be taken as an indication of the fact that there is a growing demand for a knowledge of even such a phase of popular Indian faith as represented by the belief in the existence of spirits and spirit-world recognized and engrafted in Buddhism. It is indeed a matter of great satisfaction to me that I have got an opportunity of bringing out a second edition embodying the results of my further study of the subject in a new light. The interest of this little book remains unabated in spite of the subsequent publication of my *Heaven and Hell in Buddhist Perspective* in 1925 with Professor B. M. Barua's thoughtful and informative account of the *Books of Stories of Heaven and Hell* included in the Appendix. Sir Charles Eliot points out that the belief in the existence of departed ancestors and the presentation of offerings to them have always formed a part of Hindu domestic religion and, to gratify this persistent belief, Buddhism recognized the world of *petas*, i.e. ghosts or spirits (*Hinduism and Buddhism*, vol. i, p. 338). On a careful analysis of all the *Peta* stories in the *Petavatthu* and its commentary, I find that what Sir Charles Eliot has said is a truth, but not the whole truth. It will be seen that the *Peta* stories, as presented in the *Petavatthu*, are so devised as to serve the Buddhist purpose which is no other than claiming and establishing the superiority of Buddhism as a religion, changing the mode of expression of sorrow felt in the human heart, diverting the attention of the people from the belief to pious action, and giving an incentive to moral life by making the pictures of heavenly enjoyment brighter by means of a contrast with those of varying degrees of suffering in the *Petaloka* and other forms of hell. Thus the emphasis has been sought to be shifted from the belief itself to the need of self-improvcment through moral rectification and to that of piety and benevolence, religion, and higher life. It will, moreover, be seen that already before the rise of Buddhism the happy Vedic conception of *pitṛloka* yielded its place to the pathetic Brahmanic notion of *pretaloka*, the woeful world of *Pretas*, ghosts, or spirits. And it was in this Brahmanic phase that the belief gradually found its way into Buddhism. The Buddhist treatment of the subject leaves us rather in the dark as to the connection between the two worlds, though there are several indications to suggest that there is no impassable barrier between the one and the other. The general trend of the Brahmanical Hindu belief is that the *Pretas* on their release from the state of woe go to fill the rank of the *pitaras* or "fathers". The Buddhist position, on the whole, is that, whether believers or unbelievers in *paraloka*, the practice of offering *dakkhiṇā* in honour of or for the benefit of the dead ancestors or kinsmen is fruitful if it is done in a right spirit and in a proper form.

In the general sense, the *Pretas* are those who are dead and gone and pass either as happy dead or as unhappy dead. The stories of the first are to be found in the *Vimānavatthu,* and those of the second in the *Petavatthu* with certain exceptions to the rule. The term "spirits" is used in this treatise to denote the unhappy dead who suffer in the nether world on account of their misdeeds in a previous existence.

BIMALA CHURN LAW.

43 KAILAS BOSE STREET,
CALCUTTA.
March, 1936.

CONTENTS

CHAPTER I

Pretas AND *Pitaras*

PETA which is a Pāli form of the Sanskrit *preta* literally means "he who has gone forth", "he is completely gone herefrom", "the departed one", and hence "the departed spirit of a dead person" as Childers puts it.[1] In the Pāli expression *petānaṁ kālakatānaṁ*,[2] the word *peta* occurs as a synonym of *kālakata*, "he who has expired the term of his life, "he who has died".[3] The verbal form *pecca* (Sk. *pretya*) literally means "having gone here from", and by implication "having gone to the next world".[4] It is usually employed antithetically to *idha* (here, in the present existence).[5] So if *idha* means "here", "this world" (*ihaloka*), *pecca* must be taken to mean "hereafter" (*paratra*), "the next world" (*paraloka*). The idea of *pecca* is expressed by the oft-recurring phrase *kāyassa bhedā parammaraṇā*,[6] "on the dissolution of the body, after death." Thus *Peta* and *pecca* carry

[1] *Dictionary of the Pāli Language*, 378.
[2] *Dīgha*, iii, 189.
[3] *Manorathapūraṇī*, Siamese ed., ii, 512: *Petā 'ti kālakatā*; iii, 406: *petā ti maccubhāvaṁ gatā kālakatā ti matā.*
[4] Ibid., 181: *petassa ti paralokaṁ gatassa*; 409: *pecca = paralokaṁ gantvā.*
[5] *Dhammapada*, 3. *Yamakavaggo*, verse 15: *Idha socati, pecca socati, pāpakarī ubhayattha socati, so socati, so vihaññati, disvā kammakiliṭṭhaṁ attano.*
[6] *Dīgha*, iii, 96. Cf. *Bṛhadāraṇyaka Up.*, iv, 15, 13: *na pretya saṁjñāsti tyare bravīmi.* Here *pretya* simply means "after death".

the idea of destiny (*gati*) of an individual after death. The said destiny is also expressed by the word *abhisamparāyo*, "the sequel to the event of death."[1] If the destiny is a happy one it is called *sugato* or *suggati*, and if it proves to be otherwise it is called *duggati*.[2] The moral factor which determines the destiny is *kamma-vipāka*, "the maturity of one's own deed, of one's own action." The subject of *peta* or *preta* is, therefore, bound up with the problem of existence of the next world (*paraloka*).[3]

The verbal correspondence between the Pāli *peta* and the Vedic *pitṛ* is evident from the word *petti-visaya* or *pitti-visaya* which is just another name for *petaloka*, "the world of the *pitaras* or *pretas*." The *pitaras* or "fathers" are in one sense *pubbapetas*,[4] "those who have died before," and by implication "the kinsmen who have passed into the next world". The same verbal correspondence between *peta* and *pitṛ* may be established by the parallelism between the Gṛhya list of five *mahāyajñas* and the Pāli list of five *balis*, the *mahāyajñas* and the *balis* constituting the five essential duties of a cultured householder.[5]

[1] *Dīgha*, ii, 91 : "*Sāḷho nāma bhante bhikkhu Nādike kālakato, tassa kā gati, ko abhisamparāyo?* The *Upaniṣad* term is *sāmparayāḥ*."

[2] *Majjhima*, iii, 210.

[3] *Kaṭha Up.*, i, 20 : *Yeyaṁ prete vicikitsā manuṣye : (a) stīty eke, nāyam astīti caike* "The doubt which prevails among men about *Preta* (the next world, hereafter) : Some say it exists, some say it does not exist."

[4] *Manorathapūraṇī*, Siamese ed., ii, 408 : *Pubbapetānaṁ = paralokagatānaṁ ñātakānaṁ* ; iii, 37–8 : *pubbapetānan ti paralokagatānaṁ*.

[5] *Manu*, iii, 69–71.

Five *mahāyajñas* : *brahmayajña*, *pitṛyajña*, *devayajña*, *bhūtayajña*, and *nṛyajña*.[1]

Five *balis* : *ñātibali*, *atithibali*, *pubbapetabali*, *rājabali*, and *devabali*.[2]

Here *pubbapetabali* corresponds with *pitṛyajña*; *ñātibali*, *atithibali*, and *rājabali* correspond with *nṛyajña*, and *devabali* with *brahmayjña* and *devayajña*.[3] According to the *Manusaṁhitā*, the *pitṛyajña* consists in *tarpaṇa* or offering of oblations which constitutes the essential feature of the performance of *śrāddha*.[4] According to Buddhism, the *pubbapetabali* consists in the ceremonial offering of *dakkhiṇā*.[5]

It is characteristically observed in the *Pāli-English Dictionary* : "The Buddhistic *peta* represents the Vedic *pitaraḥ* (*Manu*, cf. *pitṛyajña*) as well as the Brahmanic *preta*. The first are souls of the 'fathers', the second ghosts, leading usually a miserable existence as the result (*kammaphala*) or punishment of some former misdeed (usually avarice)."

The connection between the Buddhistic *petas* and the Vedic *pitaras* is not clear except in the verbal correspondence between the Pāli *petti* or *pitti* on the one hand and the Vedic *pitṛ* on the other. The connection may, of course, be established if both *petas* or *pubba-petas* and the *pitaras* be taken in a general sense to mean "those who have died before," irrespective of the destiny after death. For even,

[1] *Manu*, iii, 70, etc. [2] *Aṅguttara*, iii, 45.
[3] *Manu*, iii, 70 :—
Adhyāpanaṁ brahmayajñaḥ, pitṛyajñastu tarpaṇaṁ |
homo daivo, balir bhanto, nṛyajño 'tithi-pūjanaṁ ||
[4] *Manu*, iii, 81 : *pitṝñchrāddhena*.
[5] *Dīgha*, iii, 66.

according to the Vedic Funeral Hymn (RV., x, 15 and 54), the *pitaras* are " those who have departed earlier and later " (*ye purvāsaḥ, ye uparāsaḥ iyuḥ*), " those burnt with fire and not burnt with fire " (*ye agnidagdhāḥ, ye anagnidagdhāḥ*).[1] But as regards their destiny after death, they are " the blessed dead who dwell in the third heaven or highest step of Viṣṇu ". Macdonell clearly describing the happy state of the Vedic *pitaras* says that the original ancestors followed the ancient paths and the seers made the paths for the recent dead to join them. The *pitaras* are classed as higher, lower, and middle, as earlier and later who though not always known to their descendants are known to *Agni*. They revel with *Yama* and take their food with the gods. They are fond of *Soma* and they have thirst for the libations prepared for them on earth. They come on the same car as Indra and the gods. They range themselves on the sacrificial grass to the south and drink the pressed draught. They protect their worshippers. They are invoked to give riches, children, and long life to their sons who desire to be in their good graces. Thus they are said to have adorned the sky with stars, to have placed darkness in the night and light in the day. The path trodden by the fathers (*pitriyāna*) is different from that trodden by the gods (*devayāna*).[2]

[1] The original meaning of *preta* may be easily deduced from the Vedic Funeral Hymn in which the dead man is urged to " go forth by those ancient paths on which the fathers of old have passed away " :—

prehi prehi pathibhiḥ pūrvebhi
yathā naḥ purve pitaraḥ pareyuḥ.

[2] *A Vedic Reader for Students*, 176. Cf. Ragozin's *Vedic India*, 177.

With the Buddhists the *Petas* are dead kinsmen (*ñātakā, ñātī*): the happy dead or the unhappy dead. Those who are virtuous have a happy destiny after death and attain to the condition of the *devas* or gods, and those who are vicious have an unhappy destiny and attain to the condition of the *vinipātikas* or fallen. The latter include the *Petas*, narrowly so called the inhabitants of *pettivisaya* or *petaloka.* As there are varying degrees of happiness in the various forms of heaven, so there are varying degrees of misery in the various forms of hell (*niraya*), better purgatory. The *devas* of the six lower heavens of lust (*cha kāmāvacara-devā*), as described in Buddhism, are owners of celestial mansions or cars (*vimānas, rathas*). The occasional appearance of the *devas* and the occasional apparitions of the *petas* on earth are not denied. The offering of *balis* establishes the bond of affection between the living and the dead. Sometimes two separate words, *ñātī* and *sālohitā*, are employed to denote all kinsmen,[1] the first being taken to mean all relatives on the side of wife[2] and the second to mean all relatives on one's own side, i.e. all persons and forefathers with whom, both on the side of father and on that of mother, one is connected by the same blood.[3] But a set of three terms, *ñāti*, *mitta*, and *suhajja*, the Asokan *mitra, saṁstuta*, and *ñāti*,[4] is also used to exhaust all personal relations. The idea of kinship is infinitely widened in the *Metta-sutta* or

[1] *Aṅguttara*, i, 139.

[2] *Manorathapūraṇī*, Siamese ed., iii, 406: *petā ti maccubhāvaṁ gatā, ñātī ti sassu-sasurapakkhikā.*

[3] Ibid., 406: *Sālohitā ti ekalohitabaddhā pitāmahādayo.*

[4] *Rock Edicts*, iii and xi.

Karaṇīyametta-sutta[1] to include the entire world of existence or the entire universe of life, either known or unknown, actual or possible. For all practical purposes, the range of kinship by the same blood is carried back to the seventh degree, on the paternal as well as the maternal side (*satta pitāmaha-yugā, satta purisa-yugā*).[2]

The Buddhistic *petas*, in the narrow sense of the term, are, like the Vedic *pitaras*, the dwellers of *pettivisaya* or *pitṛloka*; they too are beings who belong to the next world, the world of *Yama* (*pāralokikā-sattā, Yamalokikā*).[3] But the Vedic *pitṛloka* is an upper world[4] while the Buddhistic *pettivisaya* or *petaloka* is a nether world.[5] The Vedic *pitaras* are the blessed dead, while the Buddhistic *petas* are *vinipātikā*, the downfallen. The Vedic *Yama* is the kindest protector of the fathers, while the Buddhistic *Yama* is the fiercest object of the dead, the terrible deity who sits in judgment and punishes the sinners after their death. In the Vedic Funeral Hymn (RV., x, 14), the dead man is urged to proceed thus: "Go forth, go forth by those ancient paths on which our fathers of old have passed away. Thou shalt see both kings rejoicing in the offering to the dead, *Yama* and *Varuṇa* the god; and also: Begone, disperse, slink off from here: for him the Fathers have prepared this place. *Yama* gives him a resting place distinguished by days and waters and nights."[6]

[1] *Khuddaka-Pāṭha*, P.T.S., 8–9.
[2] *Dīgha*, i, 113; ibid., iii, 5.
[3] *Petavatthu*, ii, 1: "*petīmhi duggatā Yamalokikā*."
[4] *Bṛhadāraṇyaka Up.*, iv, 3, 33. [5] *Petavatthu*, iv, 11.
[6] *A Vedic Reader for Students*, 169–170.

In the same Vedic Funeral Hymn, the two dogs of *Yama*, the sons of *Saramā*, the four-eyed brindled dogs (*catuḥ akṣān śabalān*), are viewed as "the guardians, four-eyed watchers of the path, observers of men, broad-nosed, life-stealing, who as messengers of *Yama* wander among men, while in Buddhistic description the two dogs, *Savala* and *Sāma*, big-bodied, strong and powerful, devour the sinners who, having deceased from here, fall into the purgatory in the next world, with their teeth as strong as steel.[1]

Like the Vedic *pitaras* whose seats are allocated to the south (*dakṣiṇato niṣadya*), the Buddhistic *petas* are placed in the southern quarter (*dakkhiṇaṁ disaṁ*) which is guarded by *Virūḷha* the *Lokapāla*, the lord of the *Kumbhāṅḍas* (*Kuṣmāṇḍas*). But how are the *Petas* described in the *Āṭānāṭiya-Suttanta*? They are described outright as "back-biters and murderous brigands, crafty-minded rogues, thieves and cheats." [2]

The Brahmanical claim of the existence of the *devas* and *pitaras* and of the world beyond (*paraloka*) as people call it finds its echo in the *gāthās* of the *Jātaka*.[3]

[1] *Mahānārada-kassapa-Jātaka*, Fausböll, No. 544 :—
Sabalo ca Sāmo ca duve suvāṇā,
pavaḍḍhakāyā balino mahantā,
Khādanti dantehi ayomayehi
ito panuṇṇaṁ paraloka pattan'ti.

[2] *Dīgha*, iii, 197–8 :—
Yena petā pavuccanti
pisuṇā piṭṭhi-maṁsikā
pāṇātipātino luddhā
corā nekatikā janā,
Ito 'sā dakkhiṇā disā'
iti naṁ ācikkhati jano.

[3] Fausböll, *Jātaka*, vi, 245 :—
Atth'eva devā pitaro ca atthi loko paro
atthi jano yaṁ āhu.

CHAPTER II

FIRST EXPRESSION OF THE *PRETA*-BELIEF IN BUDDHISM

IT is certain that Buddhism did not create the *Preta*-belief. The belief in its varying forms was already there in the country, among the people at large,[1] and served as the basis of many religious and philosophical controversies,[2] as well as of many social functions and religious rites. It also found its expression both through literature and art. It was given a distinct place in the domestic religion of the Indo-Aryan people, as Gṛhya system of the Brahmanical teachers. The guiding principle of practical Buddhism not to introduce anything which is inconsistent with the existing tradition of the time and not to upset that which is well established as a custom,[3] the belief itself and the social functions and religious rites based upon it were recognized as a matter of course. The regular offering of *peta-dakkhiṇā* (gifts in honour and for the sake of dead ancestors) is enjoined as a duty

[1] Barua, *Gayā and Buddha-Gayā*, vol. i, 266.

[2] *Pāyāsi-Suttanta, Dīgha*, iii; *Jaina Rāya-Paseni*; B. C. Law's *Heaven and Hell in Buddhist Perspective*, Appendix; *Mahānāradakassapa-Jātaka* (F. No. 544).

[3] *Dīgha*, ii, 74: "*Yāvakīvañ ca Ānanda Vajjī apaññattam na paññāpessanti, paññattam na samucchindissanti, yathā paññatte porāṇe Vajjidhamme samādāya vattissanti, vuddhi yeva Ānanda Vajjīnaṁ, pāṭikaṅkhā no parihāni.*"

of the cultured householder who is the inheritor of ancestral property.[1]

The five *mahāyajñas* came to be recognized as the five essential duties of an Aryan householder, especially of one who was a Brahmin by birth. The *Brahmayajña* consisted in the study and teaching of the *Veda*, the *pitṛyajña* in the offering of oblations, the *devayajña* in the performance of *homa*, the *bhūtayajña* in animal sacrifice, and the *nṛyajña* in hospitality.[2] Almost corresponding to these *mahāyajñas*, the Buddha is said to have recommended the practice of five *balis* as essential duties of an Aryan householder who is a lay follower. The five duties consist in the fulfilment of one's obligations to one's kinsmen, to the guests, to the departed ancestors and kinsmen, to the king, and to the gods and godly men.[3] The same is differently expressed thus : " When a good man is born in a family, he lives and works for the benefit, good, and happiness of many a person, father and mother, wife and children, slaves and servants, friends and relatives, dead kinsmen and ancestors, the reigning king, the gods and divinities, and all men of religion—the *Śramaṇas* and *Brāhmaṇas*. He who thus lives and functions, well established in the good faith and overcoming avarice which blackens human nature, attains to *śivaloka*.[4]

[1] *Aṅguttara*, iii, 43 : "*dāyajjaṁ paṭipajjati atha vā pana petānaṁ dakkhiṇam anuppadassati.*"

[2] *Manu*, iii, 70 : *Adhyāpanaṁ brahmayajñaḥ, pitṛyajñastu tarpanaṁ homo daivo, balir bhanto, nṛyajño' tithi-pūjanaṁ.*

[3] *Aṅguttara*, iii, 45.

[4] *Aṅguttara*, iv, 244–5 : *Sappuriso bhikkhave kule jāyamāno bahuno janassa atthāya hitāya sukhāya hoti, mātāpitunnaṁ,*

The notion of a scale of beings in the upper grade, from men upwards, and of measures of happiness enjoyed in different sub-grades is met with in the *Bṛhadāraṇyaka Upaniṣad* (iv, 3, 33), in the words of *Yājñavalkya.* If the total amount of happiness by the best of average men be the unit of measurement, a hundred of such units taken together constitute the average of happiness enjoyed by *Pita* of the *Pitṛloka.* A hundred of units determined by the total amount of happiness enjoyed by the best of the Fathers, taken together, constitute the average of happiness enjoyed by a *Gandharva* of the *Gandharvaloka.* The scale is gradually raised in this manner from the *Gandharvaloka* to the *Karmadeva,* from the latter to the *Ājānadeva,* from the *Ājānadevaloka* to the *Prajāpati,* and from the *Prajāpatiloka* to the *Brahma,* the sinless and passionless *Śrotriyas* among men alone being entitled to the highest measure of happiness in the *Brahmaloka.*[1]

This notion implied by way of an antithesis another notion of a scale of beings in the lower grade, from men downwards, and of degrees of misery suffered in different sub-grades which developed subsequently and presumably before the rise of Buddhism. This was evidently a logical

puttadārassa, dāsakammakaraporisassa, mittāmaccānaṁ, pubbapetānaṁ, rañño, devatānaṁ, samaṇabrāhmaṇānaṁ atthāya hitāya sukhāya hoti.

Sabbesaṁ sa hito hoti saddhamme suppatiṭṭhito
vineyya maccheramalam sa lokam bhajate sivam.

[1] *Sa yo manuṣyānaṁ rāddhaḥ samṛddho bhavatyenyesāṁ adhipatiḥ sarvair mānuṣyakair bhogaiḥ sampannatamaḥ sa manuṣyānāṁ parama ānando 'tha, ye śataṁ manuṣyānāṁ ānandaḥ sa ekaḥ pitṛṇāṁ jitalokānāṁ ānando.*

development of thought and imagination which proceeded from the law of *karma*, the credit for the first clear formulation of which is due to *Ṛṣi Yājñavalkya*, the sage and philosopher of *Videha*.[1] " *Ātman* the ultimate reality being all that is and all modalities of existence being possible in *ātman*, *kāma* (passion) or *akāma* (passionlessness), *krodha* (wrath) or *akrodha* (amity), *dharma* (piety) or *adharma* (impiety), the cosmic law is that a person becomes as he acts or behaves, if he acts well, he fares well, if he acts ill, he fares ill, he becomes virtuous by the acts of virtue and vicious by the acts of vice." [2]

The teaching of *Uddālaka Āruṇi* in the *Chāndogya Upanishad* suggests a ninefold division of matter (3 by 3) according to three *Guṇas*, expressed in terms of three colours, each *Guṇa* being manifest in three degrees or forms of development, viz. the grossest (*sthaviṣṭha*), the intermediate (*madhyama*), and the subtlest (*aṇiṣṭha*).[3] This afterwards became the historical basis of the nine-fold divisions of beings after death according to three *Guṇas* (qualities of action), each manifests in its three modes of expression, *adhama*, *madhyama*, and *agrya*. A clear description of this with illustrations is to be found

[1] Barua's *History of Pre-Buddhistic Indian Philosophy*, 177.

[2] *Bṛhad Ār. Up.*, iv, 4, 5: " *Sa vā ayaṁ ātmā Brahma vijñānamayo manomayaḥ prāṇamayaś cakṣurmayaḥ śrotramayaḥ pṛthivīmaya āpomayo vāyumaya ākāśamayas tejomayo 'tejomayaḥ kāmamayo 'kāmamayaḥ krodhamayo 'krodhamayaḥ dharmamayo 'dharmamayaḥ sarvamayas tad yad etad idammayo 'domaya iti yathākārī yathācārī tathā bhavati, sādhukārī sādhur bhavati pāpakārī papo bhavati, puṇyaḥ puṇyena karmaṇā bhavati pāpaḥ pāpena.*"

[3] *Chāndogya Up.*, vi, 4, 5.

in the concluding chapter of the extant *Manu-saṁhitā.* The same ninefold division of destinies of beings after death must have been in the immediate background of the Buddhist conception of *nava sattāvāsā*, the nine abodes of beings or conditions of existence. Any how, the gradation of beings, as recognized in the mythology of early Buddhism or as explained and illustrated in the Pāli commentaries, is substantially the same as in the *Manu-saṁhitā.* The gradation of beings is briefly set forth in the following words in the *Petavatthu* (iv, 11) :—

Diṭṭhā tayā nirayā tiracchānayonī
Petā asurā atha vā pi manussā devā.[1]

" Thou hast seen the purgatories, the animal-births, the *Pretas*, the *Asuras*, the average human beings and the *Devas* (gods and angels)."

The gradation of beings, implied in the Buddhist conception of *nava sattāvāsā*, is thus described in the *Dīgha-Nikāya* (iii, p. 263) and other works [2]: " There are beings who are diverse in bodily forms and in minds, such as some classes of men, some classes of gods, and some classes of the fallen (*vinipātikā*). This is the first abode. There are beings who are diverse in bodily forms but uniform in mind, such as the *Brahmakāyika* deities. This is the second abode. There are beings who are uniform in body but diverse in minds, such as the *Ābhāsvara* deities. This is the third abode. There are beings who are uniform in body and mind, such

[1] Cf. *Aṅguttara*, i, 37 ; v, 269–270, etc.
[2] *Khuddakapāṭha-Commentary*, 86–7.

as the *Subhakṛtṣṇa* deities. This is the fourth abode. There are beings who are unconscious of mundane experience, such as the *Asaṁjñasattva* deities. This is the fifth abode. The next four abodes are represented by beings who dwell in the four realms of infinity, Space, Cognition, Nothingness, and Neither Consciousness nor Unconsciousness."[1]

The *Manu-saṁhitā* describes the threefold course of transmigration that depends on the three qualities, each discriminated as threefold, low, middling, and high, according to the peculiar nature of the acts and thoughts of men in the following words:—

"Immovable beings, insects, both small and great, fishes, snakes and tortoises, cattle and wild animals, are the lowest conditions to which the quality of Darkness leads.

"Elephants, horses, *Śūdras,* and despicable barbarians, lions, tigers, and boars are the middling states, caused by the quality of Darkness.

"*Cāraṇas, Suparṇas* and hypocrites, *Rākṣasas* and *Piśācas* belong to the highest rank of conditions among those produced by Darkness.

"*Jhallas, Mallas, Naṭas,* men who subsist by despicable occupations and those addicted to gambling and drinking, form the lowest order of conditions caused by Activity.

"Kings and *Kṣatriyas,* the domestic priests of kings, and those who delight in the warfare of disputations constitute the middling rank of the states caused by Activity.

[1] *Sant'āvuso sattā nānatta-kāyā nānatta-saññino seyyathā pi manussā ekacce ca devā ekacce ca vinipātikā,* etc.

" The *Gandharvas*, the *Guhyakas*, and the servants of the gods, likewise the *Apsarases*, belong all to the highest rank of conditions produced by Activity.

" Hermits, ascetics, *Brāhmaṇas*, the crowds of the *Vaimānika* deities, the lunar mansions, and the *Daityas* form the first and lowest rank of the existences caused by Goodness.

" Sacrificers, the sages, the gods, the *Vedas*, the heavenly lights, the years, the manes, and the *Sādhyas* constitute the second order of existences caused by Goodness.

" The sages declare Brahmā, the creator of the universe, the Law, the Great One, and the Undiscernible One to constitute the highest order of beings produced by Goddness." [1]

In the tradition of early Buddhism, the *Preta*-belief and the religious rites and social functions based upon it are generally found associated with the Brahmins. In the *Matakabhatta-Jātaka* (F. No. 18), for instance, a Brahmin is said to have thought of preparing a sumptuous periodical feast in honour or for the sake of the dead kinsmen and ancestors by sacrificing a ram. The Birth-story describes how the ram was washed first with the holy waters of a river and adorned with the five-finger-marks before it was taken to the place of execution. Secondly, in the *Aṅguttara-Nikāya* (v, pp. 269 foll.), it is in reply to a query, from the great Brahmin teacher *Jāṇaśruti* (Pāli, *Jāṇussoni*) of *Śrāvastī*, that the Buddha is said to have expressed the following opinion :—

The *Pretas* subsist on food that they obtain in the

[1] *Manu*, xii, 41–50. *The Laws of Manu* (S.B.E.), 493–5

Pretaloka, the world of departed spirits, or that is offered to them by their friends, associates, relatives, and blood-relations. If a *Preta*, for whose sake the offering is made, does not perchance come to receive and enjoy it, then another *Preta* who is expecting such an offering profits by it, it being impossible in the nature of things that the *Pretaloka* shall ever be denuded of its dwellers.[1] But even assuming that there is no *Preta* to receive the offering made, yet the act of offering is not fruitless inasmuch as the giver himself derives somehow some benefit therefrom.[2]

In the *Anguttara Nikāya* (iii, 6), the Buddha says, in the spirit of Brahmanism indeed, that the parents normally desire to have sons in the expectation that they will make offerings to them when they become *pretas*.[3] The same authority propounds that those among the cultured householders who are pious and charitable are of service both to their living kinsmen and to the departed ones who have become *pretas*.[4] The *Nimi-Jātaka* (F. No. 541) says that *Sāgara*, *Mucalinda* (*Mucakunda*), *Bhagīrasa* (*Bhagīratha*), and a few others among

[1] *Yo pettivisayikānaṁ sattānaṁ āhāro, tena so tattha yāpeti, tena so tattha tiṭṭhati, yaṁ vā pan'assa ito anuppavecchanti mittā vā amaccā vā ñāti vā sālohitā vā, tena so tattha yāpeti. . . . Sace pana so peto ñāti-sālohito taṁ ṭhānaṁ anupapanno hoti. . . . Aññe pi'ssa brāhmaṇa petā ñāti-sālohitā taṁ ṭhānaṁ upapannā honti. . . . Aṭṭhānaṁ kho etaṁ brāhmaṇa anavakāso yan taṁ ṭhānaṁ vivittaṁ assa. . . .*

[2] *Api ca brāhmaṇa dāyako pi anipphalo.*

[3] *Aṅguttara*, iii, 43 : *Pañc'imāni ṭhānāni sampassantā mātāpitaro puttaṁ icchanti kule jāyamānaṁ : Bhato vā no bharissati, kiccaṁ vā no karissati, kulavaṁso ciraṁ ṭhassati, dāyajjaṁ paṭipajjissati, atha vā pana petānaṁ kālakatānaṁ dakkhiṇaṁ anuppadassati.*

[4] *Aṅguttara*, iii, 43.

the former kings had to go to the *Pretaloka* on account of their sins in spite of the fact that they were noted for their charity.[1] In the *Vessaṇtara-Jātaka* (F. No. 547), one reads of the *pretas* as a class of beings suffering pain and misery in the *Pretaloka* as a consequence of their sinful acts.[2] On the other hand, the *Nimi-Jātaka* speaks of *Yāma-hanu*, *Somayāga*, *Manojava*, *Samudda*, *Bharata*, and a few others among the ancient sages who passed beyond the *Preta-bhavana* by virtue of the practice of *brahmacariya* (holy life).[3]

The *Bālapaṇḍita-Sutta*, addressed to the *Bhikkhus*, gives a definition of one who is a fool, as well as a definition of one who is wise and contrasts the results of the action of the first with those of the action of the second. A fool is defined as one who thinks an evil thought, utters an evil speech, and does an evil deed. He is certainly a wicked man who causes harm to life, takes what is not his own, commits adultery, indulges in lying speech, and is addicted to the use of intoxicants. A wise man, on the other hand, is defined as one who thinks a good thought, utters a good speech, and does a good deed. He is indeed a good man who abstains from causing harm to life, and the rest, and is pious, virtuous, sober, and the like. The *Sutta* next proceeds to mention the different kinds of punishment a fool is bound to suffer in this life on account of his misdeeds, as well as the different animal births and the social grades of such untouchables among men as *nesādas*, *caṇḍālas*, *pukkusas*, *rathakāras*, and the

[1] *Jātaka*, vi, 99–101.
[2] *Jātaka*, vi, 595.
[3] *Jātaka*, vi, 99.

rest. Similarly it mentions the various rewards of good deeds done by a good man on the earth, and tells us how a happy destiny follows after death, entitling him to an existence in different heavens.[1]

The *Devadūta-Sutta,* also addressed to the *Bhikkhus,* bases the whole discourse on the doctrine of *karma* on the current popular belief about *Yama* and his messengers called *devadūtas* or timely warnings. It represents *Yama* as the lord of the nether world whose business it is to sit in judgment over the actions of different sinners as they are brought under arrest by his men to his court. He is the person who maintains different purgatories (*nirayas*), carefully guarded by the warders, to punish the sinners after their death for their moral rectification. It mentions the various purgatories or hells by name and describes the ruthless manner of punishing those whose lot it is to suffer there. The five messengers or timely warnings mentioned are: (1) the development of the thinking faculty with the age; (2) the appearance of the signs of old age, decay, and decrepitude; (3) the periodical occurrence of diseases; (4) the various forms of punishment meted out by the king's order to those who are found guilty of criminal action; and (5) the ghastly sight of dead bodies undergoing the process of decomposition in a charnel field. It is claimed that the Buddha himself distinctly saw by his divine intuition how the individual beings rose up and fell from state to state, some being reborn in a state of happiness, some in a state of woe, all

[1] *Majjhima-Nikāya,* iii, 163 ff.

according to their good or bad deeds, the destinies following after their death.[1]

The persons, men or women, have a happy destiny after death who are endowed with good conduct as regards the body, the speech, and the mind, who do not speak in dispraise of the elect, whose views are well-directed, and who follow actions in accordance with those views. And those men or women have an unhappy destiny after death who are depraved by bad conduct as regards the body, the speech, and the mind, who speak in dispraise of the elect, whose views are ill-directed, and who follow actions in accordance with those views[2]

Thirdly, the *Cūḷakammavibhanga-Sutta*, addressed to the young Brahmin Scholar *Śubha*, is highly important as formulating in the clearest possible terms the doctrine of *karma* which is substantially the same as that in the *Bṛhadāraṇyaka Upaniṣad* already referred to. The doctrine is stated thus :—

Kammassakā, māṇava, sattā kammadāyādā kammayonī kammabandhū kammapaṭisaraṇā, kammaṁ satte vibhajati yadidaṁ hīnappaṇītatāyā ti.

" The beings, O Brahmin youth, have the *karma* as their own, they have their heritage from the *karma*, the *karma* determines their birth, the *karma* is their friend and ultimate refuge, and it is the *karma* that divides them, relegating them either

[1] In the *Bhayabherava-Sutta*, *Majjhima*, i, 22–3, this kind of knowledge, the *sattānaṁ cutūpapātañāṇa*, is called *vijjā*, a special faculty which was developed by the Buddha.

[2] *Majjhima*, iii, 178 ff. According to *Aṅguttara*, v, 270, the unhappy destiny after death includes rebirth in the *Pettivisaya* or *Petaloka*. *Idha ekacco pāṇātipāti hoti, adinnādāyī hoti, . . . abhijjhālu hoti, Vyāpannacitto hoti, micchādiṭṭhiko hoti, so kāyassa bhedā parammaraṇā Petti-visayaṁ upapajjati.*

to the inferior or to the superior state of existence."

All that precedes or follows consists only of details without bringing any new idea.[1]

The tradition of Buddhism resents throughout the disbelief, in all its shades and grades and forms, as to the existence of the next world (*paraloka*), the existence of heavens and hells (*sagga-niraya*), the possibility of reward and retribution following invariably on men's action, good or evil (*sukata-dukkaṭānaṁ kammānaṁ phalaṁ vipāko*), the possibility of inter-communication between this world and the next, and the utility of the religious rites and social functions for the sake of the dead. The bold utterance of atheism (*nāstikya*), thus understood, is simply dreaded.[2] It also rejects all philosophical doctrines, typically those associated with *Ajita Kesakambalī, Pāyāsi, Pūraṇa Kassapa, Pakudha Kaccāyana, Makkhali Gosāla, Sañjaya Belaṭṭhiputta,* and others, which in the Buddhist estimation (and so also in the Jaina) either contradict, or do not bear out, or at least fall short of the truth of the doctrine of *karma.*[3]

Along with the promulgation of the doctrine of *karma* and the development of the idea of heavens and hells, the Buddhist teachers developed an argument to prove the futility of weeping either as a means of bringing back the dead person to life or even as a dignified mode of expression of sorrow

[1] *Majjhima,* iii, 202 ff.

[2] *Dhammapada, Lokavagga,* verse 176 :—
" *vitiṇṇaparalokassa n'atthipāpaṁ akāriyaṁ.*"

[3] *Sāmaññaphala-Sutta* (*Dīgha,* i) ; *Mahākammavibhaṅga-Sutta* (*Majjhima,* iii) ; *Mahānāradakassapa-Jātaka* (Fausböll, *Jātaka,* vol. vi).

felt in the human heart. This argument has been clearly set forth in as many as four *Jātakas*, the *Sujāta* (F. No. 352), the *Matarodana* (F. No. 317), the *Ananusociya* (F. No. 328), and the *Maṭṭakuṇḍalī* (F. No. 449), all conveying one and the same moral.[1] The Bharhut illustration of the *Sujāta* story goes to prove that this argument developed as early as the second century B.C., if not still earlier.

[1] Barua, *Barhut*, bk. i, *Stone as a Story-Teller*, 91.

CHAPTER III

Formal Expression of the Belief

THE *Preta*-belief found its formal expression in the *Petavatthu*, the Book of Stories of Hell. It consists of four *vaggas* (groups, parts) : the *Uraga*, the *Ubbarī*, the *Cūḷa*, and the *Mahā*, the first comprising 12 *Vatthus*, the second 13, the third 10, and the fourth 16. A *Vatthu* is a story, actually related or merely implied. The *Vatthus*, as presented in the *Petavatthu*, are mostly personal testimonies borne by the pretas themselves. Thus the stories have generally assumed the form of so many autobiographies of the *Pretas*, and the *Petavatthu* stands as a Buddhist Book of the Dead. But the majority of the *Pretas* introduced in the *Petavatthu* are the unhappy dead, those who are dwellers of the *Pettivisaya* or *Petaloka*—the spirits or ghosts who form by themselves a class of infernal beings.

The term *vatthu* has been consistently treated as a story by *Dhammapāla* in his *Paramatthadīpaṇī*, a commentary on the *Petavatthu*. But the term, as employed in the text itself, does not invariably mean a story. The *Vatthu*, called *Tirokuḍḍha*, which forms the doctrinal basis of *Peta-dakkhiṇā* (offerings to the dead), is appropriately called a *Sutta* or Discourse in the *Khuddakapāṭha*. The Discourse must have been current among the Buddhists in the third century B.C., as may be proved by the half of its stanzas, cited in the *Kathāvatthu*.[1] The *Petavatthu* and the *Vimānavatthu* have a common nucleus in the three *Vatthus* called the *Serissaka*, the *Maṭṭhakuṇḍalī*, and the *Revatī*. The former, as shown by Dr. Barua, may be chronologically later than the latter, both having a common historical basis in the *Pāyāsi-Suttanta*, a prose Discourse in the *Dīgha-Nikāya*, with its Jaina counterpart in the *Rāya-Paseṇi-Sutta*.[2] Even according to the internal evidence, the *Serissaka* story, forming, as it does, a common basis of both the Books, the *Petavatthu* and the *Vimānavatthu*, is at least a century later than the Buddha's demise.[3]

Now, turning to the *Petavatthu*, one will find that the expressed purpose of the book as a whole, as stated in the very first *Vatthu*, the *Khettūpama*, is to establish the superior merit of making gifts to the Buddhist Holy Order and their efficacy as a means of releasing the *Pretas* from their state of woe :—

Khettupamā arahanto dāyakā Kassakūpamā
bījūpamaṁ deyyadhammaṁ ogho nibbattate phalaṁ.
Oghabījaṁ Kasīkhettaṁ petānaṁ dāyakassa ca
taṁ petā paribhuñjantī dātā puññena vaḍḍhati.
Idh'eva kusalaṁ katvā pete ca paṭipūjayaṁ
saggañ ca kamati ṭhānaṁ kammaṁ katvāna
bhaddakan ti.

" The holy saints are to be compared to the

[1] *Kathāvatthu*, vii, 6.
[2] B. M. Barua, *Books of Stories of Heaven and Hell*.
[3] B. C. Law, *Heaven and Hell in Buddhist Perspective*, Appendix by Dr. B. M. Barua, pp. xii ff.

extensive field of merit, the givers to the cultivators, the gifts and offerings to the seeds, and the efficacy to the harvest resulting from the down-pourings of rain-water. The seeds nurtured by rain-water in the cultivated field of merit bear fruits to both the dead kinsmen and the giver, the departed spirits enjoy the fruits, and the giver too prospers with merit. Performing a meritorious deed here in relation to the living kinsmen and the religious institutions and honouring the dead as well, the pious giver proceeds to heaven after having done a good deed on the earth."

The Buddha or the supremely Enlightened One is naturally represented as the highest object of veneration. Below him is allowed to stand the holy order of the good men (*sappurisā*), the saints (*arahantā*), or noble disciples (*ariyasāvakā*) occupying the eight spiritual ranks and constituting the four pairs of noble men. Other *religieux,* other men of religion, the *Śramaṇas and the Brāhmaṇas,* are not excluded from the list of persons worthy of honour, veneration and liberality, though the predilection is sought to be created in favour of the members of the Buddhist Holy Order. The real point to be considered is whether or no the persons to whom the gifts are made are worthy of them. In Buddhist opinion, liberality should be shown discriminately and not indiscriminately. So one reads in the *Aṅkura-Preta* story (PV., ii, 9) :—

" In all the ten thousand horizons of the World system the gods and angels assembled to worship the supremely Enlightened One. There is no god or angel who can surpass him in glory, while the supremely Enlightened One surpasses in glory all of them taken together."

The god *Aṅkura* said to *Indra* who took the former to be most shining among the deities :—

" Just as if on a high and barren land many seeds were planted, it does not yield a rich harvest, nor does it gladden the heart of the cultivator by the fruit it bears, just so if many gifts be placed for acceptance by persons of dubious morals, those gifts do not produce ample merit, nor do they gladden the heart of the giver by the fruit they bear. Just as, on the other hand, if even a small quantity of seeds were sown on a fertile land, a rich harvest fills up the granary, gladdening the heart of the cultivator, just so if even a small measure of honour were done to virtuous men endowed with the quality of character, a large measure of merit results from it, being nurtured by a good rainfall. Accordingly the gift should be made discriminately, where it will produce a great fruit, because it is by discriminate charity that the giver proceeds to heaven. The discriminate charity is highly praised by *Sugata*. Those who are really worthy of honour and gifts in the world of men, the gifts should be made to them, for the gifts thus made bear a rich fruit, just as the seeds do when they are sown in a suitable soil." [1]

The same *Vatthu* distinguishes between the

[1] *Petavatthu*, 28 :—
Viceyya dānaṁ dātabbaṁ yattha dinnaṁ mahapphalaṁ
Viceyya dānaṁ datvāna saggaṁ gacchanti dāyakā.
Viceyya dānaṁ sugatappaseṭṭhaṁ (? *-pasatthaṁ*), *ye dakkhiṇeyyā idha jīvaloke*
etesu dinnāni mahapphalāni bījāni vuttāni yathā sukhette.

charity dispensed by a person with one's own hand and from one's own store and the charity made to be dispensed by others with their hands and from their stores, and opines that the merit which results from the latter kind of charity by far outweighs that which results from the former. It also discourages excesses in both the act of giving and that of not giving. It praises saving better than charity.[1]

A number of *Vatthus* are devised to restrain men and women from evil thought, evil speech, and evil action towards the *religieux* in general and the Buddhist recluses in particular, as well as to encourage them in showing a good mind, uttering a good word, and doing service to all holy men. The psychological effect on the mind of the hearers is sought to be heightened and intensified throughout by introducing a sharp contrast between the unhappy consequences of the one and the happy results of the other. In the *Vatthu* (i, 9), the wife of a man is said to have been reborn as a *Petī*, subsisting on dirt and filth, pus and blood, not only because she was mean-minded and miserly by her nature but also because, whilst her husband gave anything out of faith, she scolded and cursed him, bringing upon herself the very same fate which she desired to be his after death.

In the next *Vatthu* (i, 10), a pious lady reborn as a goddess, shining in glory in her celestial mansion, proclaims how, by having offered out of

[1] *Petavatthu*, 26 :—
Adānam atidānañ ca na pasaṁsanti paṇḍitā,
tasmā hi dānā dhanam eva seyyo,
samena vatteyya sa dhīradhammo.

faith as a Buddhist lay woman an overflowing oil-pot to a saintly *Bhikkhu*, upright in his conduct, she was reborn in that happy state.

In the next *Vatthu* (i, 11), the happy and glorious destiny of some members of a family who were liberal in their gifts to all men of religion, the *Śramaṇas* and *Brāhmaṇas*, is sharply contrasted with the unhappy and pathetic destiny of other members who had not done any act of merit by way of piety in spite of their large fortune and riches.

The *Vatthus* are thus manipulated and placed in all groups and sections, harping on the same tune, and emphasizing the efficacy of merit earned by liberality and so forth to all *religieux*, detailing the items of gift, and delineating the different modes of honouring and worshipping them.[1]

Even apart from the *religieux*, there are persons who are deserving of charity and liberality. They are the *yācanakā* or men and women who are indigent, helpless, and destitute. It is equally the bounden duty of a noble householder, especially one who is rich and well-to-do, to give away a portion of their wealth and earnings for those unfortunate people. Those who do not give anything in charity having means to do so, and those who spurn out the beggars from their doors or cavil at those who give, suffer consequences after death in the *Petaloka*. So the regret is put into the mouth of some of the departed spirits :—

Santesu deyyadhammesu dīpaṁ nākamham attano.[2]

[1] Cf. *Petavatthu*, ii, 1 ; ii, 2 ; ii, 4 ; ii, 8 ; ii, 9 ; ii, 10 ; iii, 2 ; iii, 5 ; iii, 6 ; iii, 10 ; iv, 1 ; iv, 3 ; iv, 8 ; iv, 9 ; iv, 12 ; iv, 16.
[2] *Petavatthu*, 66.

" I had not made an island for me in spite of having enough to give away."

The argument in favour of charity and liberality is stated in these words :—

Yaṁ dadāti na taṁ hoti, deth'eva dānaṁ datvāna ubhayaṁ tarati ubhayaṁ tena dānena gacchati, jāgaratha mā pamajjatha.[1]

" The gift that is made may not reach the world for which it is meant, and yet give away the gift, for by giving a man overcomes the misery both here and hereafter, and attains happiness in both the worlds, doing good to oneself and to others. So be awake and be not slothful."

A householder has equally a duty to those who are dead and gone, fathers and forefathers (*pitā, pitāmahā*), friends and relatives, especially to those who are reborn in a state of woe, in the *Petaloka*, to wear out the effects of sin. It is the bounden duty of even a recluse or an ascetic, if the *Preta* waiting for release from his or her state happens to be a parent or a kith and kin. The text contains a complete Discourse, the *Tirokuḍḍa-Sutta*, stating the argument in favour of offering *dakkhiṇā* in honour and for the sake of the departed spirits :—

" The departed spirits revisiting their old homes stand behind the boundary wall of the homestead, at turnings, or where four cross-roads meet, even by the door-posts. When there is a great feast with an ample provision of food and drinks, nobody remembers the wretched beings, such being their unhappy lot due to their misdeeds. Only those among the kinsmen who are really compassionate

[1] *Petavatthu*, 67.

make from time to time an offering of eatables and drinkables that are pure, wholesome, and excellent, wishing thus : 'Let these be the share of the dead kinsmen, let them be happy.' The departed kinsmen come and, assembling there, heartily approve of the noble act, and bless : 'May our good kinsmen live long by whose piety we receive all these. They have done us a great honour, and they have not given things in vain.' "

In the *Pretaloka,* there is no agriculture, no cattle-breeding, nor is there any trade or commercial transaction. By all that is given from here the spirits live there. Just as rain-water flows down from a high level, in the same way that which is given from here rolls down to the *Pretas.* Again, just as the rivers flowing down overfill the sea, in the same way that which is given from here reaches the *Pretas.* " Whilst alive, they gave much to me, did much for me, they were my friends and associates, comrades and relatives, the offering should be made to them, remembering what they themselves had done for a person before. Neither weeping, nor sorrow, nor other forms of lamentation will be of any advantage to them, should the kinsmen who are alive be doing all these. But the gift which is made to the Holy Order is well established in it, and turns out to be of benefit to them for a long time to come, and reaches them. By this act, a social service is done to the living kinsmen, a great honour is also done to the departed spirits, the strength too is given to the *bhikkhus,* and as for yourselves, no mean joy of merit you gain." [1]

[1] *Petavatthu,* 4–5.

Dāna includes other items of meritorious work, the acts of public utility, the philanthropic deeds. As notable examples of such deeds, we have mention of a free supply of drinking water to the thirsty, the sinking of wells, excavation of tanks, and the like, and the construction of bridges,[1] the acts of merit that were specially dear to *Aśoka's* heart.

After *dāna* one has to think of *sīla*, the moral state and behaviour of the self. Morality consists in the purity of thought, speech, and action, and immorality is sin (*pāpa*) committed by way of thought, word, or deed. Morality develops from the practice of self-restraint (*saññama*), and immorality results from want of restraint, propriety, and moderation. The violation of the moral precepts both on the part of a householder and on that of a recluse is frankly stated to be a cause of unhappy destiny of a person after death, and the observance of those precepts is regarded as a means of securing a happy destiny. Envy, jealousy (*issā*), meanness (*macchariya*), back-biting (*piṭṭhimaṁsana*), and the rest are the immoral qualities of a person that bring about an unhappy destiny. These and the precepts are taken one by one, in their various aspects and varying degrees of importance, for illustration in different *Vatthus*. Some *Vatthus* describe the miserable fate of hunters who live by killing or causing harm to living beings. Some describe a similar fate of others who commit murder or are instrumental in causing death to human beings. There are some

[1] *Petavatthu*, 25 :—

Papañ ca udapānañ ca dugge
saṁkamanāni cā ti.

Cf. ibid., 20.

Vatthus that describe the fate of persons guilty of theft, robbery, dishonesty, use of false weights, and the rest, while some describe the fate of persons guilty of adultery or unchastity. Some describe the fate of persons who indulge in lying speech, calumniation of others, harsh and offensive language, and vain talks, while some *vatthus* describe the fate of persons who indulge in the drinking of liquors and the use of intoxicants. " Commit no sin either by way of thought, or speech, or action " is the emphatic word of wisdom.[1] The effect of the moral lesson sought to be conveyed is heightened by the contrast in the reward of moral life and action obtained by different persons after their death in various heavens.

False belief or wrong view of life (*micchā-diṭṭhi*) is to a great extent responsible for immoral behaviour of men. Such belief or view of life, combined with a sinful heart, immoral conduct, meanness, and speaking ill of good men, brings about the downfall of men.[2] The false belief or wrong view of life finds its expression in such utterances as follows :—

" There is no happy result or consequence of liberality or self-restraint. There is no teacher who can control an uncontrollable person. All persons, whether virtuous or wicked, are equally situated. Manly energy or effort has no meaning at all. Piety

[1] *Petavatthu*, iii, 7 :—

Mākāsi pāpakaṁ kammaṁ, mā tāta duggatiṁ agā

Cf. ibid., 55, where the moral exhortation is :—

Pāṇātipātā viramassu khippaṁ
loke adinnaṁ parivajjayassu
amajjapo mā ca musā abhāsi,
sakena dāreṇa ca hohi tuṭṭho.

[2] *Petavatthu*, 20, 59.

does not purify a sinner. Fate alone determines the course of life. There is no mother, no father, no brother, no world hereafter, and consequently there is no offering, no oblation that may give benefit to a person after death. He who kills a man or he who beheads another, cannot thereby do harm to the soul which is of such a nature as not to be subject to destruction. Just as a man coming out of one locality enters another, or just as a man leaving an old house enters a new one, in the same way the soul leaving one old and worn out body puts on a new body. All, whether wise or fools, make an end of suffering by going through a course of transmigration, during 84,000 great cycles of existence." [1]

Hence the word of wisdom is :—

" Seeing and hearing, believe, O men, that such are the different consequences of good and evil deeds. Had there been no difference in results between good and evil, there would have been no happy or unhappy destiny of individuals after their death, or distinction among men as superior and inferior." [2]

There are five *vatthus*, the *Goṇa* and the *Uraga* put in Group I, and the *Maṭṭakuṇḍali*, the *Kaṇha*, and the *Ubbarī* put in Group II, each of them putting

[1] *Petavatthu*, iv, 3, 24–33.

[2] *Petavatthu*, iv, 1, 26–7 :—

Disvā ca sutvā abhisaddahassu
kalyāṇapāpassa ayaṁ vipāko,
kalyāṇapāpe ubhaye asante
siyā nu sattā sugatā duggatā vā
No c'ettha kammāni kareyya maccā
Kalyāṇapāpāni manussaloke
nāhesuṁ sattā sugatā duggatā vā
hīnā paṇītā ca manussaloke.

forward an interesting argument of its own stating the reason why a man or a woman should not have recourse to lamentation as an expression of sorrow for the dead, while the *Tirokuḍḍavatthu* (i, 5) definitely declares :—

Na hi ruṇṇaṁ vā soko vā yā c'aññā paridevanā,
na taṁ petānaṁ atthāya evaṁ tiṭṭhanti ñātayo.

"Neither weeping, nor sorrowing, nor other modes of lamentation turn out to be of any advantage to the dead should the kinsmen stand in that position of mourning." The *Goṇapetavatthu* (i, 8) seeks to bring us home to the truth that if it is not possible to enable the carcass of a cow to rise again to life by feeding it with grass, it is still less possible to bring back to life the dead person whose body has been completely destroyed by burning it.

The *Uragapetavatthu* (i, 12) characteristically says :—

"Just as a snake moves on casting away its old worn out skin, in the same way when a dead man is dead leaving behind his aged body, he, while being burnt in a funeral pyre, does not know of the lamentation on the part of his living kinsmen ; he fares according to his destiny. He came from there without any fear, and is gone from here without waiting for permission, as he came so is he gone, so what does lamentation mean ?" [1]

The popular idea of transmigration of soul or

[1] "*Urago' va tacam jiṇṇaṁ hitvā gaṇhati san tanuṁ,*
evam sarīre nibbhoge pete kālakate sati.
Dayhamāno na jānāti ñātīnaṁ paridevitaṁ,
tasmā evaṁ na socāmi, gato so tassa yā gati.
Anabbhito tato agā. nānuññāto ito gato,
yathāgato tathāgato, tattha kā paridevanā."

personality as illustrated by the simile of a snake moving on after casting away its old worn out skin is reproduced without any adverse comment.[1]

The *Maṭṭakuṇḍalipetavatthu* (ii, 5) and the *Kaṇhapetavatthu* (ii, 6) teach that if it is not possible to bring down on earth the sun and the moon which are visible to the eye, it is far less possible to bring back to life the dead who have passed the human ken ; it is impossible that, once born, a person shall not die. It is somewhat interesting to note that *Kṛṣṇa* the highest Hindu divinity ever possible in man is represented as a person who stood in need of such an instruction.

Lastly, the *Ubbarīpetavatthu* (ii, 13) bases the instruction on the following argument :—

"Some eighty-six hundred thousands of kings, all *Brahmadatta* by name, have been burnt on this burning ground, whose death dost thou mourn. I have been born and reborn as women, men, and sometimes as animals, no limit to the course of transmigration is to be seen, even though I have gone through a long round of births and rebirths in the past."

Thus it may be shown that all the different trends of thought which are met with in other portions of the *Pāli Canon* were brought to bear upon the Buddhist teaching in the *Petavatthu*. The popular

[1] This is substantially the same simile as that of a person entering one locality or habitat after coming out of or leaving another, viewed with disfavour in the '*Nandikāpetavatthu* (iv, 3) :

Yathā gāmato nikkhamma aññaṁ gāmaṁ pavisati
evam evaṁ pi so jīvo aññaṁ kāyaṁ pavisati.
yathā gehato nikkhamma aññaṁ gehaṁ pavisatı
evam evaṁ pi so jīvo aññaṁ bondiṁ pavisati.

beliefs are nowhere violently interfered with, nor are seriously challenged the arguments on which those beliefs were made to rest. The main underlying motive of all the *Vatthus* is to improve the mode of expression of sorrow, to encourage piety among men, to inculcate the importance and value of moral conduct, to establish the truth in the law of *karma*, and, above all, to urge all men and women to cherish faith in the Holy Triad and mould their lives according to the principles of Buddhism.

CHAPTER IV

PHYSICAL DESCRIPTION OF THE *PRETAS*

THE *Aṅguttara-Nikāya* speaks of four lying postures, the first being called *Petaseyyā*, the posture of the dead. Lying flat on the back is the general posture of the dead.[1] The *Pretas*, whose physical description is to be given here, are not simply persons who are dead and gone but those who after their death are reborn in the *Pettivisaya* or *Petaloka*. They are beings who have had an unhappy destiny after death and belong to a nether world—a realm of *Yama* (*duggatā Yamalokikā*).[2] As represented in the *Petavatthu*, they figure as so many human beings, gifted with human voice and giving vent to human feelings and sentiment. The state of existence in which they find themselves or in which they are seen by others is a pitiable condition.

In the *Vatthu* called *Sūkarapeta* (i, 2), the *Preta* concerned is introduced as a being with a golden complexion and having at the same time the physiognomy of a pig (*sūkaramukho*). The ugly face of the *Preta* was due to want of restraint in speech, while the brightness of complexion resulted from the restraint practised in action.

[1] *Aṅguttara*, ii, 244 : *Yebhuyyena petā uttānā senti.*
[2] *Petavatthu*, i, 6 ff.

In the next *Vatthu* called *Pūtimukhapeta* (i, 3), the *Preta* figures as a being who put on a divinely handsome appearance, so far as the body was concerned, but he showed a cancered mouth from which came out a stinking smell. The loathsomeness of his mouth was due to calumniation and lying speech in which he had indulged, while the glory of his bodily appearance resulted from the practice of *tapas*.

In the third *Vatthu* called *Pañcaputtakhādakapeta* (i, 5), the *Preta* is introduced as a female spirit, nude, ugly looking, emitting a foul smell, issuing forth filth, swarmed with flies. Her heart was burning and fuming with hunger and thirst, and yet she had not a drop to drink. The only food on which she was subsisting was the flesh of her dead son, mixed with blood and pus. This pitiable condition of the female spirit was due to a twofold sin committed by her: (1) bringing about miscarriage in the rival wife of her husband, and (2) taking a false oath to consider guilt.

In another *Vatthu* called *Mahāpesakārapeta* (i, 9), the *Preta* is made to appear as a female spirit subsisting on filth, blood, and pus. Even a new piece of cloth, as soon as it was offered to her, turned into a rag. Such was the distinct consequence of her cursing others to the same effect.

In the *Khalātyapeta-Vatthu* (i, 10), the *Preta* is represented as a female spirit appearing in a celestial mansion (*vimāna*), out of which she could not come as she knew that she was nude, covered only with the hair of her head. The celestial dwelling was a happy result of a gift made by her with a clean mind to the recluses and her nudity was due to some sin committed by her.

The *Nāgapeta-Vatthu* (i, 11) presents a dramatic scene of five persons—two parents, two sons and a daughter, the elder son going ahead on the back of a wild elephant, the younger son going in a chariot drawn by mules, the daughter being carried in a palanquin, illumining all quarters with her beauty, while the parents as *Pretas* followed them with clubs in their hands, weeping, their bodies maimed all over, hurting each other and subsisting on the wound-bled pus. The happy state of the children was a palpable reward of virtue, while the pitiable condition of the parents resulted from their meanness.

In the *Saṁsāramocakapeta-Vatthu* (ii, 1), the female spirit concerned is described as a being, nude, ugly looking, lean, thin, and emaciated, clothed without any flesh and blood, and dying of hunger and thirst. This pitiable condition resulted from having none, whether father or mother or a kinsman, to persuade her to show liberality to holy men.

In the next *Vatthu* (ii, 2), the female spirit represents herself as a mother of the venerable *Sāriputta* in her previous birth. As a spirit, she, tormented by hunger and thirst, subsisted on all sorts of filth and dirt, the exudations of a dead body burning on a funeral pyre and similar substances that she could procure, blood or pus from a human or an animal body. She had no other habitat to dwell in but the ash-covered terrace on a funeral ground. Such was her destiny brought about by her sinful deed.

In the *Nandāpeta-Vatthu* (ii, 4), the female spirit figures as a veritable *Kālī*, with an ugly appearance, terrific in looks, purple-eyed, and having sharpened teeth. This terrible condition was due to her harshness in nature and angry speech.

In the *Uttaramātupeta-Vatthu* (ii, 10), the *Preta* concerned appears as a female spirit who lived on the bank of the Ganges. She was ugly and terrific in looks, nude but covered all over her body with a bushy growth of hair that hanged down to the level of her feet. During the fifty-five years since her death she knew not what food or drink was. Though the mighty Ganges flowed down before her eyes, the waters, as soon as she touched with her hand, all turned into blood. Such was the cruel fate of her former sin.

The *Kaṇṇamuṇḍapeta-Vatthu* (ii, 12) introduces a female spirit destined to enjoy and suffer alternately. In her turn of enjoyment she appeared in all her glory and splendour as a most fortunate goddess in her delightful heavenly mansion, while, as soon as her turn of suffering came, the sight was dreadfully changed, when she was seen with her ears lopped off and surrounded by a pack of hungry hounds devouring her from all sides and reducing her to a ghastly looking bony frame. The miserable part of her destiny was of course due to her sinful deed.

In the *Abhijjamānapetavatthu* (iii, 1), the *Preta* is represented as a spirit who was seen walking in water without sinking in it, nude, wearing a garland, with his body adorned with jewelleries and without any sexual form. We are told that among the spirits, some are seen clad in rags, and some covered only by the hanging bush of hair of the head, and all run hither and thither, being driven by hunger and thirst, and obtaining nothing to eat, lie down on earth tired and exhausted.

The *Sānuvāsipetavatthu* (iii, 2) introduces some *Pretas* who appeared as lean, emaciated, and panicky, as though ailing from pin-pricks in the throat, having nothing to eat, while another spirit was seen moving alone, joining together two hands and two knees, having no cloth or garment to cover his body.

In the *Bhusapetavatthu* (iii, 4), one *Preta* is represented as a male spirit with husk burning on his head, one as a female spirit with her head bleeding due to self-caused wounds, and a third as a female spirit eating food that changed into filth as soon as it was touched by her hand.

In the *Vatthu* called *Seriṇīpeta* (iii, 6), the female spirit is represented as describing her condition thus: "Thirsty, I approach a river, and it becomes at once dried up; oppressed by heat I approach a shade, and it forthwith turns into a furnace. Hot wind begins to blow burning my body."

The next two *vatthus*, called *Migaluddapeta* and *Dutiyaluddapeta* (iii, 7, 8), describe the pitiable condition of two *pretas*, both of whom were in their previous birth professional hunters, enjoying happiness by night and suffering torments in a cemetery or the like.

The *Kūṭavinicchayakapetavatthu* (iii, 9) speaks of a *preta* who was seen eating the flesh of the back part of his body although he appeared otherwise to be a very fortunate being. As may be easily imagined, his fate was due to his back-biting habit combined with other depravities.

In the next *vatthu*, called *Dhātuvivaṇṇapeta* (iii, 10), the *preta* appears as a being who remained standing in the air, emitting bad smell out of his cancerated mouth, and causing wounds on his thigh with a sword held in his hand.

In the *Ambasakkharapetavatthu* (iv, 1) the *preta* is described as a being without any shelter, comfort and joy, having nothing to eat or to drink. He is seen regretting his miserable fate, brought about by his own misdeeds in the past.

The *Nandikāpetavatthu* (iv, 3) speaks of a *māyā* created by a *preta*. A path appeared in front without its continuation behind. Unnatural smell was being scented and terrific sounds were being heard and a banyan tree was looking like a tower of clouds. He made his appearance in the guise of a god richly attired and adorned with jewelleries. He extended his hospitality to the king of *Suraṭṭha*, requesting him to eat cakes and drink all sweet drinks.

In the *Ucchupetavatthu* (iv, 5) the *preta* describes his pitiable condition in these words : " I constantly feel as if sharpened sugar-cane leaves are cutting my throat inside. Oppressed by hunger, I fall down on earth. Hungry and tired, thirsty and deprived of joy, I roll like birds during hot summer.

The *Gūthakhādakapetavatthu* (iv, 8) speaks of a *preta* as a spirit who was seen coming out of a heap of filth on which he subsisted.

In the *Gaṇàpetavatthu* (iv, 10), the *preta* gives the following description of his miserable state : " Thirsty, I walk into a river which becomes at once dried up. Oppressed by heat I approach a shade which forthwith turns into a furnace. Hot winds begin to blow burning my body as though in blazing fire. I wander about many *yojanas* in search of food, and return utterly disappointed. Overcome by hunger I lie down prostrate on the ground, dropping as a dead man."

The *Manu-saṁhitā* speaks of an *Ulkāmukha preta* who subsists on what has been vomited; a *Kaṭaputana preta* who eats impure substances; a *Maitrākṣajyotika preta* who feeds on pus; a *Cailāśaka preta* who feeds on moths: The men of four cases who have fallen off from their respective duty become such *pretas* in order.[1]

Mrs. S. Stevenson has shown that in the popular Hindu belief, a *preta* has a throat as narrow as the eye of a needle, so it can neither drink water nor breathe, and its shape is such that it can never stand or sit, but it is ever flying in the wind. A man who commits suicide becomes either a *preta* or a *bhūta* (ghost), a *preta's* time being spent in unrelieved misery. A sacrifice (*prāyaścitta-homa*) is to be performed for the purification of a *preta* from any of the thirty-two ritual sins that the dead man may have committed whilst dying, such as accidentally touching an unclean thing at the time of death, dying on a bedstead without being shaved or not being bathed before death. The priest recites two different *mantras* so that the dead man's *preta* may be delivered from its disembodied state.[2]

Spence Hardy, basing his account on the later

[1] xii, 71–2.

[2] *The Rites of the Twice-born*, 191, 199.

Pāli legends, says: " The inhabitants of the *Lokāntarika naraka* are *pretas*. Their bodies are 12 miles high, and they have very large nails. On the top of the head there is a mouth about the size of a needle's eye. In the world of men there is a *preta* birth called *Nijhāmātaṇhā*. The bodies of these *pretas* always burn. They continually wander about, never remaining in one place a longer period than the snapping of a finger. They live thus an entire *kalpa*. They never receive food or water and weep without intermission.[1] The Pāli tradition also speaks of other kinds of *pretas* known as *Khuppipāsas*, having heads 144 miles in size, tongues 80 miles long, with the body thin and extremely tall. There are also the *Kāḷakañjakas*, who continually chase and maim each other with fire and shining weapons. There is another class of *pretas* called *Utūpajīvī*, subsisting on the warmth of the seasons.[2]

[1] *Manual of Buddhism*, 58.
[2] Childers, *Dictionary of the Pāli Language*, 379.

CHAPTER V

PRETA–STORIES

IT was left to the commentator of the *Petavatthu* either to supply the *preta*-story which is implied in a *vatthu* or to develop the story which is briefly sketched in the canonical text. The stories must have been in the process of formation long before the time of *Dhammapāla*, to whom one owes the extant Pāla Commentary on the *Petavatthu*. The Pāli version presupposes a Singhalese Commentary in which the stories must have taken a definite shape. Similar stories may be found here and there, in later Buddhist works. Three of the stories in *Dhammapāla's Paramatthadīpanī* are found to be in agreement with those in the *Dhammapada Commentary*, wrongly ascribed by tradition to *Buddhaghosa*.

The *preta*-stories, as narrated in *Dhammapāla's Commentary* are no doubt important especially as supplying a context to each of the *vatthus*. The stories are being briefly presented, and the reader may take them for what they are worth.

1. *Khettūpamapeta*

This *peta* was, in his previous birth, the son of a very wealthy merchant of *Rājagaha*, the capital of *Magadha*. He was the only son of his parents, who thought that if he had spent even a thousand coins every day he would not have been able to exhaust their wealth. With this thought in their mind they did not care to teach him any art (*sippa*), and when he came of age they married him to a damsel who had no faith in the Buddha or in his doctrine. Enjoying life with her, he spent his days, and after his parents' death he surrounded himself with rogues that cheated him of his money. He spent his wealth in enjoyment and merry-making, giving away liberally to musicians, actors, and others of the same class without doing any acts of merit. At last he became so poor that he could not make both ends meet and lived as a beggar in the public almshouse (*anāthasālā*) in the same city. One day a band of robbers met and advised him to take to robbery and theft along with them. He joined their gang and was caught in the very first expedition with them before he could steal anything. The king ordered him to be beheaded. While he was being taken to the scaffold, a beauty of the town named *Sulasā* was moved at the wretched plight of the once rich and liberal young man and entreated the officers to wait a moment as she wanted to give him some sweets to eat and water to drink. At that time *Mahāmoggallāna* thought of going there to offer him an opportunity of acquiring merit at the last moment of his earthly existence. He went there with his alms-bowl. The banker's son offered him sweets and the drink brought by *Sulasā*. After this he was beheaded. By virtue of the great merit acquired by his gift to *Mahāmoggallāna*, he deserved to be reborn in the great *devaloka*, the blissful abode of the gods ; but at the last moment, at the thought that he was indebted to *Sulasā* for this timely opportunity of making a gift, his heart was filled with affection towards her, with the result that he was born on a much lower plane, as a tree-spirit residing on a banyan tree. Owing to this attachment, he stole away *Sulasā* while she was in the garden where the deity resided by producing darkness and storm by means of his miraculous power. The deity kept her with him on the tree for a week, after the expiry of which she was left at the corner of the assembly in the *Veḷuvanavihāra* where the Buddha was preaching.

2. *Sūkaramukhapeta*

During the dispensation of Buddha *Kassapa*, a *bhikkhu*, who practised restraint so far as his body was concerned but was unrestrained in speech, used to scold and abuse his fellow *bhikkhus*. After death he was reborn in hell, but in the time of Buddha Gautama, he was born again in the *Gijjhakūṭa* near *Rājagaha*, and on account of the *kamma* that still remained to fructify, he was suffering from hunger and thirst. His body was of a golden hue, but the face was like that of a pig. The venerable *Nārada*, who lived on the *Gijjhakūṭa* hill, met him once early in the morning when he was going out on his alms-begging excursion.

3. *Pūtimukhapeta*

During the dispensation of Buddha *Kassapa*, two young men of good family who became devoted and pious *bhikkhus*, used to dwell in a village. They were fast friends. A *bhikkhu* with evil intent came, and, finding the place very comfortable and food and drink easily obtainable, wanted to have the *vihāra* for himself alone, after driving out its former occupants. He was successful in bringing about an ill-feeling between them and both of them left the place. The *bhikkhu*, who was of evil motive, died soon, suffering under the burden of his sins and was cast into the hell called *Avīci*.

The envious *bhikkhu*, after residing in hell for the period between two Buddhas, came out of it when Gautama Buddha was living on earth to wear out the residue of his sin by sufferings on earth as a *peta*, and dwelt near *Rājagaha*. The venerable *Nārada* met him while coming down from the *Gijjhakūṭa* hill and enquired: "Your appearance is beautiful, you live in the sky, but a very dirty smell comes out of your mouth and vermin are moving in it. What did you do in the past to deserve even this?" The *peta* replied, "I was a wicked monk unrestrained in speech; good appearance has been acquired by me by having outwardly kept up the semblance of a recluse, but the stench in my mouth is the sequel of my harmful words."

4. *Piṭṭhadhītalikapeta*

At *Sāvatthī* the nurse of *Anāthapiṇḍika's* grand-daughter gave her a doll. The grand-daughter played with it and called it her daughter. One day while she was engaged in sport, her doll fell down and was broken. The girl began to cry that her daughter was no more; nobody could console her and the nurse took her to *Anāthapiṇḍika* who sat by the side of the Buddha and the *bhikkhus*. *Anāthapiṇḍika* consoled her by saying that she should make offerings to her departed daughter. The Buddha was invited to a dinner next day. The Master uttered some stanzas expressing approval of the offer made by *Anāthapiṇḍika*. For whomsoever the offering is made, whether for departed relatives or for the household deity or other gods, the donor himself acquires merit and the donee is also served; sorrow, lamentation and weeping are of no use to the *petas*; these only bring suffering to the living relatives.

5. *Tirokuḍḍapetas*

Long ago, ninety-two *kalpas* back, there was a town called *Kāsipurī*, of which *Jayasena* was the king. *Sirimā* was his queen. Their son was *Phussa*, who attained Buddhahood.

The king was very affectionate to his son and he used to say: "The *Buddha*, the *Dhamma*, the *Saṁgha* are mine. I shall allow nobody else to offer the four *paccayas* (the four requisites of a *bhikkhu*) to them." The other sons of the king got no opportunity of making offerings to the Buddha and thought out a plan to obtain their father's permission. They instigated the frontier people to rise in rebellion against the king and they themselves were sent to suppress the outbreak. When they returned successful the king wanted to grant them a favour, and they would ask for no boon except permission to offer the four-*paccayas* to the Buddha and his disciples. The king reluctantly gave them permission for three months only. After making the necessary arrangements, they took the Buddha to the newly built *vihāra* and made offerings to him. Some amongst them, however, became dissatisfied, as owing to shortness of time they got no opportunity of making any offerings on their own account. The dissatisfied people put many obstacles in the way of the brothers. Sometimes they ate up the offerings and sometimes they spoiled them. They went so far as to set fire to the alms-house ; these people were reborn in hell for their misdeeds and at the time of *Kassapa Buddha*, they were reborn as *petas*. As they did not obtain any offering from their relatives, they went to *Kassapa Buddha* and asked the reason of it. They were told that they would get offerings at the time of *Gautama Buddha* during the reign of King *Bimbisāra*, who was their former relative. When King *Bimbisāra* offered the *Veḷuvana vihāra* to the Buddha and his disciples, the *petas* hoped that they would get a share of the merit acquired by *Bimbisāra*, but in vain. Consequently they made a horrible noise in the palace. Next morning, *Bimbisāra*, frightened by the din made overnight, went to the Buddha and asked him about the cause of the trouble. Buddha told him that some of his relatives in a former birth were now *petas* and hoped to be relieved of their sufferings by sharing the merit acquired by him (*Bimbisāra*), but as he did not offer anything to them they felt disappointed, and hence made the noise. King *Bimbisāra*, thus instructed by the Buddha, gave a sumptuous dinner to the whole *Saṁgha* and made over to the *petas* the merit acquired by this act of goodness. In approving of this meritorious act of the king, the Buddha preached the *Tirokuḍḍasutta*.

6. *Pañcaputtakhādakapeta*

Not far from *Sāvatthī* lived a householder who had a barren wife. His friends and relatives told him that he should marry again but this he would not do owing to the great affection that he entertained for the wife. His wife persuaded him to get another wife so that his family line might not come to an end. Urged by her, the householder took another girl as wife and brought her to his house. Shortly afterwards the second wife became pregnant. The first wife now grew jealous and she caused miscarriage with the help of a *paribbājaka*, whom she had pleased with food and drink. The parents of the second wife coming to know of the miscarriage, charged the first wife with the offence, but she denied the charge, swearing that, if she were guilty of it, she might be driven by hunger and thirst to eat up five sons both morning and evening and further suffer various other troubles. The woman was reborn not far from that village as a *petī* on account of the sin committed by her. She could not get any food or drink. She used to beat five sons in the morning and five in the evening and had to eat up their flesh and yet could not satisfy her hunger. No cloth did she get to wear. Her body emitted an unbearable stench and was full of flies and vermin. Once eight *theras* when going to the Master at *Sāvatthī* saw her in this plight and asked her what was the cause of her misery. She told them what had happened. The *theras*, moved by pity, entered the house of the householder, her former husband, who offered them food and drink and they persuaded him to offer the merit of this act of charity to his former wife, who was thus freed from her miserable condition.

7. *Sattaputtakhādakapeta*

A Buddhist householder had by his wife two sons who were good in every way. The latter, proud of her sons, used to disregard her husband, who, being offended, married again; when the second wife became pregnant, the first wife caused her to take some drug which brought about miscarriage. The sequel of this sinful act was that she was reborn in a state of woe as a *petī*.

8. *Goṇapeta*

A householder at *Sāvatthī* breathed his last. His son was overwhelmed with grief and used to go about hither and thither, asking anybody and everybody about his father and could not by any means be consoled. The Buddha, seeing his miserable condition, went to his house, when the man put to him the question whether he knew where his father was gone. The Buddha, in reply, asked whether he wanted to know of his father in this birth or in those he had in the past. In this way he pacified his troubled soul. This was not the first occasion that the Master had soothed his aching heart, but in the past also he had done the same. In the past, the father of a householder at Benares died. The man was disconsolate. His son, *Sujāta*, was a clever fellow, and thinking of some means to bring consolation to his father who was sorely afflicted, he went outside the city and found there a dead bullock in a field ; he then went to the carcass of the bullock with hay, grass and water and repeatedly asked the bullock to eat and drink. The passers-by seeing this wanted to know the reason of such a strange behaviour. The son did not answer and they went to his father and told him that his son *Sujāta* had gone mad. The father ran at once to the spot and enquired why he was behaving like a mad man. The son replied, " I am not quite sure who is mad, you or I ? I am giving food and drink to a bullock whose head and legs are here, in fact, the whole of whose body is before me, but nothing of the respected grandfather can be seen, neither his feet nor hands, nor his head, nor any other part of his body ; weeping for him of whom there is nothing left behind, it is rather you that are beside your senses."

9. *Mahāpesakārapeta*

Twelve *bhikkhus* took *kammaṭṭhāna* from the Buddha and went out in search of a suitable residence where clothes might be had. Gradually they found a beautiful forest tract and in the neighbourhood, a village where, it so turned out, lived eleven families of weavers, The weavers coming to learn that the *bhikkhus* were looking for a suitable residence to practise *kammaṭṭhāna* without any hindrance, invited them to live there and built cottages for them in the wood and the headman took upon himself the charge of supplying the necessities of two of the *bhikkhus*. The wife of the headman had no respect for the *bhikkhus*. Her husband, therefore, brought her younger sister and made her the mistress of the house. She served the *bhikkhus* with due reverence and attention. When the period of the rainy-weather-residence ended, the weavers gave a cloth to each of the *bhikkhus*. The irritated wife of the headman ridiculed her husband thus: "May the food and drink that you have presented to the *Sākyaputta* recluses be in the next world turned for you into ordure, urine, and pus, and may the clothes be changed into sheets of burning iron."

The Headman was reborn after his death as a powerful tree-god in the *Vindhya* mountain and his malicious wife, too, after her death came to live close by as a *petī*. Naked and ugly, oppressed by hunger and thirst, she came to the above tree-spirit and prayed for food and drink and a cloth to wear. He procured for her a heavenly cloth, food and drink; but no sooner did she take them than they were converted in her hands into ordure, urine and pus and the cloth as soon as worn turned into a burning sheet of iron. Suffering from anguish and extreme pain, she wandered about filling the place with her loud cries.

A *bhikkhu* after the rains was going on a visit

to the Master with some merchants through the *Vindhyāṭavi*. The merchants travelled by night and in the day time they rested in a shady retreat in the forest. One day the *bhikkhu* fell asleep and was left behind by the merchants. He wandered up and down and reached the tree where resided that virtuous spirit who, seeing him, appeared before him in human form and showed his reverence to him. At that time, the *petī*, his former wife, came and prayed for food and drink and clothes, and these the moment they were supplied by him underwent a change as described before. The *bhikkhu* asked for the reason and the tree-spirit narrated to him the whole thing and asked him whether there was any means of relief from that dreadful suffering. The *bhikkhu* answered that if food and drink and clothes were offered to a *bhikkhu* on her behalf and she at the same time heartily approved of it, then there might be a means of escape from the evil. The tree-spirit did as desired and presented two beautiful cloths to the Master through that *bhikkhu*, and thus the miserable woman was released from her wretched lot.

10. *Khalātiya-peta*

Once at Benares, there was a charming woman of the town, possessing an exquisitely fine feature and complexion. Many young men were attracted by the beauty of her hair. Some women, jealous of her hair, bribed her maid to apply some drugs that would destroy it. The maid mixed them with her bathing powder and gave it to her when she went to bathe in the Ganges. As soon as she plunged in waters, her hair fell off by the roots. Thus deprived of her hair, she looked ugly, and being ashamed to go to town, lived outside the city and made a living by dealing in oil and wine. Once she invited some people to drink wine as much as possible and when they were overdrunk, she took away their clothings. One day, seeing an *Arahat* going round for alms, she invited him to her house and served him with a choice dish prepared with oil. The *Arahat*, out of compassion for her, partook of the food thus offered, while she stood holding an umbrella over his head, which he approved. She at the same time prayed for beautiful hair. As a result of her good and evil deeds, she in her next life found herself seated alone in a golden *vimāna* (a celestial mansion) on the ocean ; she got back the beautiful hair as prayed for, but on account of her having stolen the clothings, she was naked. Thus being born again in that *vimāna*, she passed a long period, covering the interval between two Buddhas. When the present Buddha was on this earth, a hundred merchants of *Sāvatthī* saw her *vimāna* on the wide ocean while on a voyage to *Suvarṇa-bhūmi* ; their ship was being driven hither and thither by contrary winds. The chief of the merchants gazing with wonder on the golden mansion, entreated the occupant to come out. Naked as she was, she was ashamed of appearing before the merchants. He offered her upper garments (*uttarīyạ*) wherewith she might robe herself and appear before him. She replied that anything given her with hands would not reach her, and requested him to make a gift of the cloth to a pious and faithful *Upāsaka* who was on board the ship and let the effect of this meritorious deed be transferred to her. As soon as this was done and the merit accruing therefrom was given her, she came out of her mansion with a sweet smile on her face, draped in the finest garments. Struck with wonder at such a quick effect of meritorious work, the merchants enquired about her past *karmas* and these, both good and bad, she detailed to them, gave them food and drink, and requested them to take some presents to the Buddha at *Sāvatthī*, where they went and worshipped the Buddha in her name. The Lord approved of this merit and the *petī* was reborn in a golden palace in the *Tāvatiṁsa* heaven.

11. *Nāgapeta*

Saṁkicca, a seven-year-old boy, became an *Arahat*, while shaving his head. Becoming a *sāmaṇera* (novice), he was dwelling in a forest-hermitage with thirty *bhikkhus* whom he saved from the hands of 500 robbers.

He instructed the robbers in the doctrine of the Master and initiated them as *sāmaṇeras*. He took them all to the Buddha, and after listening to the teachings of the Master, they became *Arahats* and *Saṁkicca* received full ordination from the Master and came to *Isipatana* with 500 *bhikkhus*. There was a pious and faithful lay believer at Benares who used to instruct people to give alms to the *bhikkhus*.

At that time, a Brahmin had two sons and one daughter. The eldest son was a friend of the

Upāsaka. One day the *Upāsaka* came to *Saṁkicca* accompanied by the Brahmin's eldest son. The latter acquired some amount of faith in the Buddha. The *Upāsaka* advised him to offer alms daily to a *bhikkhu*; but his friend, the Brahmin's son, refused by saying that this was not the custom with the Brahmins. The *Upāsaka*, however, persuaded him to give alms to him and he would offer it to the *bhikkhus*. He consented. By and by the younger brother and the sister also acquired some amount of faith in the Buddha. All these three were engaged in making offerings to the *Samaṇas* and the *Brāhmaṇas*, but their parents were false believers and did not offer alms to anybody. Their daughter was selected as bride for her maternal uncle's son, but the son became a *sāmaṇera* or novice under *Saṁkicca*. But he used to take his meal at his mother's house. His mother always pressed him to marry the girl she had selected. He became excited and asked permission from *Saṁkicca* to give up the *brahmacariya* life, but his teacher, seeing that he would soon become an *Arahat*, asked him to wait a month. After a month he was asked to wait a fortnight and again a week more. In the meantime, the house of his bride's parents fell down, causing death to the Brahmin and his wife, two sons and daughter. The husband and wife became spirits (*peta* and *petī*), and the two sons and daughter *devatās* living on earth. The *peta* and *petī* used to beat each other with iron clubs and as the result of beating, boils appeared and burst out and the pair used to suck blood and pus from each other's boils. The *sāmaṇera* asked his teacher's permission to go home. The teacher asked him to come after sunset while the fourteenth day of the dark fortnight continued. In the meantime, the teacher went behind the *Isipatana vihāra* and waited there; at that time, the two brothers with their sister were passing by the side of the *vihāra* on their way to an assembly of the *Yakkhas* and their parents were following them in the most wretched plight, striking each other with iron clubs. *Saṁkicca* pointed this out to the *sāmaṇera*, who at his bidding asked them about the past deeds that had caused their present condition.

12. *Uragapeta*

At *Sâvatthī*, there was a Buddhist layman who had a son who died. He became mad with grief and did not pay attention to household duties; nor did he go out, as was his practice before. The Buddha knowing this, went to the house of the *Upāsaka* and related to him the *Uraga Jātaka* which runs thus :—

At Benares, there was once a Brahmin family named *Dhammapāla* and all the members of the family used to meditate upon death and if any one went out of the house, he instructed others not to lament. One day, the Brahmin went to cultivate the field accompanied by his son, who set fire to the dry grass, weeds, etc., and a black snake bit him, frightened by the fire. The Brahmin asked a passer-by to tell his wife to come to the field with rice sufficient for one man and garlands and other sweet-scented things, after she had herself bathed and put on pure garments. The passer-by went to the Brahmin's house and delivered the message. The members of the family acted according to the instruction given by the Brahmin. The Brahmin, after taking bath and meal, adorned himself with garlands, etc., surrounded by the members of the family, put the dead body of his son on a pyre, and they all sat on one side, as if nothing had happened. The Brahmin's son was himself reborn as *Sakka* in heaven and he was the *Bodhisatta.* Moved with pity, he came down in the guise of a Brahmin and asked the Brahmin, " Are you burning a deer ? If so, please let me have some meat." The Brahmin replied, "No, my young son who was endowed with all good qualities, is being burnt." " If you are burning your son, it is strange that you are not in the least moved." The Brahmin replied, " Just as an *uraga* (snake) goes away leaving behind its old skin, so a human being leaves the body without having any attachment for it. On the other hand, the body cannot conceive that it is being burnt or that the relatives are in mourning, I do not, therefore, grieve for my son who has gone where his own *karma* has led him." Then the *Sakka* turned to the mother and asked her, " Though the father may be hard, the mother who has brought up the son with so much care must have a softer heart, why is she not grieved for her child ? " She replied, " He came uncalled for and has gone away without asking for permission. He is not conscious of his body being burnt by us nor of the lamentations of his relatives, therefore, I do not cry or lament ; he is bound by his own *karma*." The god then turned to his sister and asked her, "Why are you not sorrowful, as we know that sisters feel very great affection for brothers." The sister replied, "If I were to make myself lean and thin by crying it would be of no avail; if I spoil my health by crying, the relatives would be sorry, therefore, I do not mourn for him, he has followed the path which was his own." The king of the gods turned at last to the wife and said, "A wife has great attachment towards her husband and if the husband dies, the wife becomes a helpless widow. But you do not show any such grief nor make any lamentation for your deceased husband." She replied, "Crying for a departed husband is like a child's cry for catching the moon." *Sakka* also enquired of the dead man's maid-servant, saying, "As you were ill-treated by your deceased master, now you are free from him and it is for this reason that you are not crying." She replied, "No. Although he was my master's son, yet I loved him as my own child. As an earthen pot cannot be repaired when broken, so a dead body cannot be brought to life again; it is needless to cry." *Sakka* then introduced himself to the Brahmin and other members of the family, gave them great wealth to enjoy and then left them.[1]

The Master, narrating this story to the *Upāsaka* at *Sāvatthī*, freed him from his grief and revealed to him many truths.

[1] See for Bharhut illustration of the story, Barua's *Barhut*, bk. ii.

13. *Maṭṭhakuṇḍalipeta*

Maṭṭhakuṇḍali was the son of a miserly Brahmin at *Sāvatthī*. On account of the meanness of his father, the boy could not perform any meritorious deed, except saluting the Lord with great reverence and respect. For this merit, he was born as a god; his father was mourning his death in the cemetery. He went to the cemetery in the guise of a *peta* and began to cry for the sun and the moon. The father said, "Why are you crying for the sun and the moon which cannot be got? You must be a fool to do this!" The *peta* answered, "The sun and the moon for which I am crying are visible, but your dead son for whom you are crying cannot even be seen. Then, please, judge for yourself who is the greater fool." The father's sorrow abated, and the father enquired, "Who are you?" The *peta* introduced himself to him, and manifested himself in full celestial splendour.[1]

14. *Saṭṭhikūṭasahassapeta*

There lived at Benares a cripple who could pierce anything with a stone. One of his pupils learnt the art from him and in order to test his skill in the art shot a stone which broke the head of a *paccekabuddha*, named *Sunetta*, who sat on the banks of the Ganges. The *paccekabuddha* obtained *parinibbāna* then and there. The people finding the saint dead, killed the pupil, who suffered many years in the *Avīci* hell and was reborn as a *peta* near

[1] Cf. *Dhammapada Commentary*, i, 28.

Rājagaha to wear out the remaining sin. As a consequence of his misdeeds, sixty thousand iron arrows appeared on his head three times a day, and he fell down on the ground with broken head and when they disappeared he regained his former normal state of health. One day the venerable *Mahāmoggallāna*, when coming down from the *Gijjhakūṭa* hill, saw the *peta* and had a talk with the spirit.

15. *Seṭṭhiputtapeta*

Pasenadi, the King of *Kosala*, heard four terrible sounds at dead of night, *Du-sā-nā-so*. Next morning, he sent for his chaplain, told him that he had heard such a sound and asked him what could it mean. The chaplain thinking that there was a very good opportunity for enriching the Brahmins, replied, "In consequence of this, there will be danger to your life, kingdom, or wealth; but by performing a *Sabbacatukka Yajña* you will be saved." The king then asked his officers to make arrangements. Hearing this, the Queen *Mallikādevī* dissuaded the king from performing the sacrifice entailing the slaughter of many animals and she advised him to go to the all-knowing Buddha and follow his instruction. Accordingly he went to the Master who told him that nothing would happen to the king, that those cries came from four *petas* who were suffering in the *Lohakumbhi* hell, and that those four sinners had been sons of *seṭṭhis* at *Rājagaha* in their previous birth. They were habitual adulterers. Sometimes they committed adultery by paying money to the girl, sometimes by fraud, and sometimes by enticement. In consequence of their misdeeds they were now in hell. It took them thirty thousand years to go to the bottom of the hell and the same period they took to come up to the top therefrom. Thus they came to the topmost part of the hell ; they tried their utmost to give vent to their terrible sufferings in hell and each uttered a stanza which was not heard fully, but only the first letter was audible. The Buddha repeated these stanzas fully to the king, the purport of which is as follows :—" It is now sixty thousand years that we have been suffering in hell, when will our sufferings end ? The sins committed by us are endless. We have spent our life in misdeeds. We had plenty of wealth and we misused it ; if we go from this place and become human beings, we shall accumulate much merit by charity and observance of the precepts." [1]

16. *Bhogasaṁharapeta*

When the Buddha was at *Veḷuvana*, four women used to earn money as hawkers by selling things and cheating people by using false weights, etc. They were reborn as *petīs*, residing on the wall encircling *Rājagaha*. Being overwhelmed with great pain, they used to cry loudly at night, saying, " We have accumulated wealth by fair and foul means ; others are enjoying the wealth, we are the partakers of misery only." The people hearing this became terrified and asked the Buddha, after making

[1] Cf. Fausböll, *Jātaka*, iii, 44–8 ; *Dhammapada Commentary*, ii, 10–11.

offerings to him, as to the cause of this. The Buddha said, "The sound will not put you to any inconvenience, the four *petīs* are crying on account of pain."

17. *Akkharukkhapeta*

When the Buddha was at *Sāvatthī*, an *Upāsaka* who was a resident of *Sāvatthī*, went to *Videha* with cartloads of merchandise. After selling his wares there and taking things from *Videha*, he started for *Sāvatthī*. In a forest tract, one pole of his cart broke down. A man was then passing through the forest with an axe to cut down trees. Seeing the merchant in a helpless condition, he took pity on him and after cutting down a tree, he prepared a pole out of the trunk of the tree for him, and repaired his cart. The wood-cutter, after death, became a god living on earth, who remembering his deeds, uttered a stanza in front of the house of the *Upāsaka* :—

"Charity not only gives reward in the next world but also in this; by practising charity, both the donor and the donee are saved. Awake, don't be indolent."

18. *Ambapeta*

When the Buddha was at *Sāvatthī*, a householder was reduced to poverty and his wife died, leaving a daughter only. After leaving his daughter in a friend's house, he went to trade, taking a loan of 100 *kahāpaṇas*. He soon recovered his capital together with a profit of 500 *kahāpaṇas* and while he was returning home with the money, a number of bandits seized him on the way. He threw the money in a bush and hid himself near it. The bandits took his life. After death, the trader lived there as a *peta* on account of his avarice. The trader's daughter heard the news of her father's death, sorrowful, and wept bitterly. Her father's friend in whose house she had been residing so long, consoled her and promised to bring her up like her father. She knowing her own poor condition, served the man well and wanting to perform the obsequies of her father prepared delicious rice-gruel and collected good mangoes. With these things she fed the Buddha and the *Bhikkhus* and at last prayed that the merit of this deed might be enjoyed by her father. The Master approved of this prayer and her departed father got a good house with a beautiful mango-garden having a *kalpa* tree and a nice pond and also many more excellent heavenly things. Sometime after, the merchants were going that way and stayed for a night at the place where they had been before. The *peta* appeared with a *vimāna* in the garden before some merchants of *Sāvatthī*, who were passing that way. The *peta* offered half the money that he had been guarding so long to the merchants and asked them to hand over the other half to his daughter, to pay off his debt and to enjoy the rest for her own benefit.

19. *Pāṭaliputtapeta*

Some merchants of *Sāvatthī* and *Pāṭaliputta* went to *Suvarṇabhūmi* in a ship. Now an *upāsaka* who was much attached to a woman, died of an illness and though he had done good deeds, yet after death was reborn as a *vimānapeta* on the sea on account of his attachment to this woman. Thus he was there on the sea with his heart fixed on the girl he loved, and it so happened that she also was on board the ship of the merchants. In order to see the woman whom he loved, the *peta* stopped by his miraculous powers the further progress of the ship. Wondering about it, the merchants came to know that it was the work of the *peta* and to save themselves, they put her on a bamboo raft and let it go with her. As soon as she left, the ship began to run fast towards *Suvaṇṇabhūmi*. The *peta* took her to his own residence and lived with her in happiness ; but after a year, she became anxious to leave this place and entreated him thus : " My dear, I am unable here to do anything that will benefit me in the next world, do kindly, therefore, take me to *Pāṭaliputta*." In reply the *peta* said, " You have seen hells and the animal world and many kinds of beings such as *petas*, *asuras*, men and gods, and you have seen with your own eyes the results of good and bad deeds (*kamma*) ; as requested I shall carry you unharmed to *Pāṭaliputta*. Do you perform meritorious deeds there ? " The woman replied, " You are my well-wisher. I shall perform meritorious deeds according to your instruction. I have indeed seen for myself the things you speak of." Then the *peta* went through the sky with the woman and left her in the centre of *Pāṭaliputta*, where she was received with joy by her friends and relatives as she had been given up as lost in the sea.

20. *Goṇapeta*

At *Sāvatthī*, there were a number of people who were unbelievers, unfaithful, misers, and doers of deeds according to their sweet will. After their death, they were all reborn in the *peta*-world and resided in groups near *Sāvatthī*. One day, the venerable *Mahāmoggallāna*, while going to *Sāvatthī* for alms, saw them on the way and asked, " What is the cause of your being naked, ugly and lean ? Why are you reduced to mere skeletons ? " " It is the effect of our own sinful deeds which have led us to our misery. If we go to a river to drink water, it becomes dried up and if when it is hot we sit in a cool shady place, the place becomes unbearable, the wind blows hot upon us ; oppressed by hunger we travel long distances but in vain, we fall down on the ground unable to get our hunger appeased ; for want of good deeds, we are suffering here and if we become human beings on earth, we would accumulate much merit." *Moggallāna* went to the Buddha and spoke to him about it.

21. *Gūthakhādakapeta*

In a village near *Sāvatthī*, a rich man built a *vihāra* for a *bhikkhu* who was much associated with his family. Many *bhikkhus* used to gather there from different quarters and the people of the village being very much pleased, used to give them food and drink. But that *bhikkhu* could not bear it and became very envious, and speaking against other *bhikkhus* who came there, induced the householder to abuse them.

The *bhikkhu* was reborn as a *peta* residing in the *vaccakuṭi* (the privy) of the *vihāra*, on account of this sin. The householder died and was reborn as a *peta* dwelling on the upper part of the privy. *Mahāmoggallāna* saw the householder *peta* and asked him as to the cause of his residing in such a dirty place. The householder *peta* replied, " My family priest is envious of other *bhikkhus* and he does not like that others should come to me, his *dāyaka* (supporter). Being induced by him, I abused the other *bhikkhus*. On account of this sin committed by me, I am reborn here as a *peta*. What has become of that *bhikkhu ?* " The *peta* replied, " He is reborn as a *peta* on the lower part of the privy and he serves me. We live here eating dirt, I partake of the leavings of other people's food and he lives upon mine." Having heard this, *Mahāmoggallāna* went away and informed the Buddha.

22. *Sānuvāsipeta*

In the past, there lived at Benares a king named *Kitava*. His son went to sport in the garden and while returning saw a *Paccekabuddha* named *Sunetta* going out of a house to seek for alms. The prince being puffed up on account of his princely power, thought, " How is it that the shaven-headed monk passes on without saluting me ? " Hence he became angry, and got down from the elephant. He asked the *Paccekabuddha* whether he had got any alms, forcibly snatched away the bowl from him and threw it on the ground, and it was broken to pieces. Finding that he was unmoved even after such treatment and was looking on with kindness, joy, and serenity of mind, the prince felt offended and said, " Knowest thou not that I am the son of King *Kitava*, what can you do by thus looking at me " ; and thus ridiculing him he went his way. But even on his way he was overtaken by a terrible burning sensation like that of hell-fire as a result of which he died and was reborn in the *Avīci* hell. After suffering from the hellish tortures for thousands of years during the dispensation of Gautama Buddha, he was reborn in a village of *Kevaṭṭas* or fishermen near *Kuṇḍinagara*. Remembering the sufferings in his previous births, he did not accompany the other fishermen who were his relatives, on fishing excursions ; but, on the other hand, when they left him, he used to tear their nets and threw the living fish into the tank. His relatives expelled him from the house, but one of his brothers was very kind to him. At that time the venerable *Ānanda* reached *Kuṇḍinagara* and was staying on the *Sānuvāsi* hill. The young *Kevaṭṭa* driven away by his relatives, wandered up and down and reached the place where the *Thera* was, at dinner time. Knowing him to be hungry, *Ānanda* offered him food and then learning the history of his past life, instructed him and finally conferred the *pabbajjā* (ordination) on him and took him to the Buddha who was very kind to him and as he had not done much good work, the Master entrusted to him the task of filling the water-jars of the *bhikkhus*. Seeing this, the *Upāsakas* made a regular supply of food for him. Afterwards he became a famous monk and the leader of a congregation of twelve thousand *bhikkhus*, and took his abode on the *Sānuvāsipabbata*. His relatives numbering five hundred who were killers of fish and who had acquired no merit by good deeds, became *petas* after death. His parents who were now *petas*, were ashamed to invite him personally, as they had driven him from home and so they sent to him his brother who had been kind to him before. This brother, now a *peta*, went to his saintly brother, informed him of the suffering of his parents and asked him for help. The *Thera* offered alms collected by him and his disciples, fed the *Saṅgha* with it to the merit of his parents and relatives who were *petas*, saying, "Let my relatives enjoy the fruit of this merit and let them be happy." Shortly afterwards the *petas* obtained good food and drink but no clothing. The *Thera* was again requested by the *petas* to give them clothes. He, after collecting rags and making clothes out of them, offered them to the *Saṅgha* and thereby they got clothes to wear. They also wanted a dwelling-place and the *Thera* built a hut of leaves and offered it to the *Saṅgha* and the *petas* got good houses. The *petas* afterwards got good conveyances. All the *petas* then came nicely dressed to worship the *Thera*.[1]

23. *Kumārapeta*

Two sons of a king of *Kośala* were very handsome in their youth and being proud of youth and beauty, they committed adultery and were reborn as *petas* residing on the moat surrounding *Kośala*. They used

[1] Cf. *Rājaputtapetakathā*.

to set up a tumult at night and the people who heard their cries, got frightened. To avert the evil effects of their cries, they made plentiful-offerings to the *Saṅgha* headed by the Buddha. Then they informed the Buddha of the object of their offerings. The Blessed One assured them that these cries would do no harm to them. The Buddha related the above story to them and asked them to transfer the merit of the offerings to the *petas*.

24. *Dhātuvivaṇṇapeta*

After the demise of the Lord, his relics were divided. *Ajātaśatru*, the king of *Magadha*, got a share of them which he enshrined with great respect and honour and then instituted a worship of the same. Thousands of people worshipped the relics. At that time some believers in false doctrines became dissatisfied and were eventually reborn as *petas*. At *Rājagaha* lived a wealthy householder whose wife, daughter, and daughter-in-law, who were staunch believers in the Buddha, went to worship the relics, taking with them sweet-scented flowers and perfumes. The wealthy householder asked them not to go to worship the relics which were mere bones and spoke in derogatory terms. But they did not pay attention to his words and went to perform their worship and returning home shortly afterwards, fell ill and passed away; after death they were reborn in the *Devaloka*, and soon after the householder also, burning with rage, died and was reborn as a *peta*. One day *Thera Kassapa* out of compassion for all, caused them for their instruction to see the *peta* and the *devatās*. The *peta* related his past history and repenting, said, " Born as a human being again, I will certainly worship the *stūpa* containing the relics of the Buddha over and over again." *Mahākassapa* made this the text of a sermon to the people.

25. *Ucchupeta*

When the Buddha was at *Veḷuvana*, a certain person took up a bundle of sugar-cane on his shoulders and walked on chewing a cane. A pious *Upāsaka* was following him along with a little boy who began to cry for a piece of sugar-cane. The father of the boy approached him and asked for a piece of sugar-cane for his son. The man with the sugar-cane sticks became angry and threw a piece of sugar-cane at him. The punishment of the man was proportionate to his deed. After death he was reborn as a *peta* and he got a sugar-cane field measuring eight *karisas*, full of very big, green, nice and juicy sugar-canes as thick as clubs. Wishing to partake of the sugar-cane, he went to the field, but as soon as he was there, the canes came down on his back and he was struck so severely that he fell down senseless. This was his lot whenever he made similar attempts. Once *Mahāmoggallāna* saw him on his way to *Rājagaha* and asked the *peta* about the cause of his suffering and the latter related to him the evil deeds done by him in his past life and the retribution that followed. The *Thera* advised him to take a bundle of sugar-cane on his back, and go to *Veḷuvana* and offer it to the

Buddha. He took a huge bundle to *Veḷuvana* and the Master with the *bhikkhu-saṅgha* enjoyed the canes and thus he got rid of his sufferings and as a result of this offering, he was reborn in the *Tāvatiṁsa* heaven.

26. *Nandikāpeta*

Two hundred years after the demise of the Lord, in the kingdom of *Suraṭṭha* there was a king named *Piṅgala*. *Piṅgala's* commander-in-chief was *Nandaka* who was a believer in false doctrines. He did not believe in happiness resulting from good deeds nor in the punishment caused by sins. *Nandaka's* daughter *Uttarā* was given in marriage to one of a family of equal position. After his death, *Nandaka* was reborn as a *peta* and resided on a banyan tree in the *Vindhyāṭavī*. His daughter, *Uttarā*, offered to a saintly *Thera* cool and perfumed drink as well as excellent cake and sweets to the benefit of her departed father, and prayed that the fruit of the merit might be reaped by him. As a result of this meritorious deed, *Nandaka* got plenty of cake and sweet drink, etc. *Nandaka* was much impressed seeing that this act of vicarious charity conferred upon him such excellent things, although he had never practised charity. He further recollected that King *Piṅgala* whose eyes had not yet opened to the true faith, had gone to a conference with King *Dhammāsoka* and would be soon coming back. *Nandaka* thought that as soon as he would see the king returning, he would speak to him and try to remove his sceptical views. Shortly afterwards the king made his appearance and the *peta Nandaka* in order to take him to his abode, led him to a wrong path which ultimately brought him to his abode. The *peta* offered the king excellent cake and good drink and fed him and his whole retinue. The king then asked him whether he was a *deva* or a *Gandhabba*. In reply, he related to him the whole of his history and told him thus, " Buddha is the foremost of all in the world of gods and men. You take refuge in *Buddha, Dhamma,* and *Saṅgha* with your wife and children. Give up killing, stealing, drinking spirituous liquors and similar other sinful habits, and be attached to your own wife." [1]

27. *Ambasakkharapeta*

When the Buddha was at *Jetavana*, a *Licchavi*, named *Ambasakkhara,* lived at *Vaiśālī*. At *Vaiśālī*, in front of a shop, there was a pit full of mud and water. The people suffered much, as they had to jump over the pit. Sometimes it happened that many fell into the pit and became covered with mud and thereby suffered considerably. The owner of the shop in order that people might have no more trouble on this account filled up the pit with bones of cattle. He was naturally pious, free from anger, and endowed with many other good qualities. One day, out of sport, without any evil intent, he concealed the garments of his associate with whom he had gone to bathe, but immediately returned the clothing to him. His nephew, however,

[1] This *vatthu* is said to have been added by the Theras of the Third Buddhist Council.

stole some articles from others' houses and concealed them in the shop of his uncle. The uncle and the nephew were arrested on a charge of theft. The uncle was sentenced to death and the nephew was placed on the stake. The merchant died and was reborn as a god living on earth and he got a good horse as a result of his good deed of putting the bones in the pit, and, for his other virtues, his body emitted a sweet scent. But, on account of his having concealed the garments, he had to go about naked. He used to go and see his nephew on horseback and bless him with the cryptic saying. "Live long, life is better." At that time the King of *Vaiśālī* named *Ambasakkhara* desired to win a beautiful damsel whom he had seen in a house in the city, while going about. Coming to know that she was the wife of another person, he engaged the husband as one of his officers in order to win the love of his wife. The husband was entrusted with the difficult task of bringing muds of red colour and a red lotus from a tank which was situated at a distance of three *yojanas* from *Vaiśālī* and the condition was that if he could not return to the city in the course of the day, he would be put to death. The husband quickly went to the tank and with the help of the spirit living in that tank, got his desired objects and reached *Vaiśālī* before sunset and before the gate was closed, but the gate-keeper, acting under the secret instructions of the king, did not allow him to go in. When on the next day, *Ambasakkhara.* wanted to take away his life, he pleaded that he had actually come in time, and cited the merchant living as a god outside the City as a witness. The *Rājā* came to the spot where the naked god was and asked him why he was naked. The god related his story and there was a long discourse between the *Rājā* and the god who exhorted him to avoid evil and do good, as every deed was sure to bring its inevitable result. The *Rājā* at last impressed by his exhortations, released the nephew of the god and he offered garments to the great *Thera Kappitaka* and to the other *bhikkhus*, in order that the naked god might obtain clothes to wear. Then the king gave up improper thoughts and deeds and took refuge in the three gems, *Buddha*, *Dhamma*, and *Saṁgha*.

28. *Kūṭavinicchayakapeta*

When the Teacher was at *Veluvana*, King *Bimbisāra* used to observe six days of fast in the month. Many persons following him also did the same. The king used to enquire of anybody and everybody who approached him whether he had observed the *uposatha*. One of his judicial officers used to speak malicious words and cheat people. He was also in the habit of taking bribes. One day the king asked him whether he had observed the *uposatha* and he answered in the affirmative, though really he had not done so. After he had left the king, he was asked why he had spoken a lie to the king. He replied that he had done so through fear. He was advised to observe the *uposatha* during the night, that he might acquire half the merit. He did so and soon after passed away from the world and as a result of his having kept the *uposatha* for a single night, he was reborn as a god with great splendour, having ten thousand damsels and obtained many heavenly things. But, on account of his using malicious words in the past life, he had to eat the flesh taken from his own body with his own hands. One day the venerable *Nārada* saw him when coming down the *Gijjhakūṭa* and asked him the reason of his being in such a wretched state. His past history was then related, as described above.

29. *Dutiyaluddapeta*

When the Teacher was at *Veluvana*, a hunter of *Rājagaha* used to hunt animals day and night. He was a wealthy man. A friend of his who was an *Upāsaka*, advised him to desist from taking life, at least at night, but he did not listen to this admonition. The *Upāsaka*, thereupon, requested a *Thera* to go to the house of his friend and teach him the "*dhamma*" that he might refrain from killing animals. The sage, one day, while wandering for alms, went to his house where he was received with great honour and respect by the man fond of hunting. Moved by his teachings the hunter gave up hunting at night. After death, he met with the same fate as *Migaluddapeta* whose story is given below.

30. *Migaluddapeta*

Migaluddapeta was a *vimāna peta*. During the day, he used to suffer much but at night he enjoyed happiness. Seeing this, the venerable *Nārada* wanted to know what he had done in his past life that he had such an unequal distribution of pleasure and pain. The *peta* said that in his past life he was a hunter at *Giribbaja* and he always used to hunt deer. One of his friends, who was a pious *Upāsaka*, unable to make him desist entirely from the slaughter of animals, at last succeeding in persuading him to abstain from it at least at night. It was this work of his that was fructifying now : in the daytime dogs were biting off his flesh as a result of his cruelty by day, while his abstinence at night made him happy after sunset.

31. *Serinipeta*

In the kingdom of the *Kurus*, at *Hatthinipura*, there lived a woman of the town named *Serinī*. In *Hatthinipura*, many *bhikkhus* came from different quarters to observe the *uposatha*. People used to serve them with various articles of food and other things. The woman who had no faith in the Buddha, and who was stingy, refused to approve the meritorious deeds done by the people and used to say that it was no good making gifts to the *Samaṇas* with shaven head. After death, she was reborn as a *petī* and dwelt close by a moat surrounding a city on the borders of the country. An *Upāsaka* of *Hatthinipura* went to the city for trade and very early in the morning before darkness had completely vanished, he went close to the moat. Having recognized him, the *petī* made herself visible, horrible to look at, naked, reduced to a skeleton ; on seeing her, he wanted to know the reason of her deplorable condition. The *petī* related to him the past history and requested him to convey the news to her mother that she was suffering in *petaloka* (the world of spirits) and that there was a large sum of money below the bedstead which she used while she was in the human world. Her mother was requested to take out the money which would enable her to get a living and she further requested her to make gifts on her behalf in order to bring about her release from that miserable plight. The *Upāsaka* informed her mother and she complied with her request and the *petī* was at last freed from the *petaloka*; she became happy and beautiful to look at and appearing before her mother, recounted to her the whole history.

32. *Kumārapeta*

At *Sāvatthī*, many *Upāsakas* joined together in a religious function and erected a very big *pandal* and decorated it beautifully. They invited the Buddha and the *bhikkhus* to come and take their seats under the canopy and after worshipping and honouring them, offered many things to the Master and the *bhikkhus*. An envious and stingy person, after seeing the worship of the Buddha, said that these things should not be given to the bald-headed ascetics, rather they should be thrown into the rubbish heap. The *Upāsakas* hearing this, said that the envious person had committed a great sin by giving vent to such feelings and induced his mother to obtain pardon for the offence. She admonished her son and at last succeeded in taking the son to the Buddha and she asked for pardon. They worshipped the Buddha and the *bhikkhus* by offering *yāgu* (rice-gruel) for a week. The son after death was reborn in the womb of a prostitute on account of his misdeeds. As soon as he was born, he was thrown by the prostitute into a cemetery, but the child, owing to its former merit, was not hurt and it was quietly sleeping there. The Buddha by his divine eye saw the child and went to the place. Many people assembled, seeing the Buddha go there. The Blessed One expounded the good and bad deeds of the child in its previous birth and predicted that the child would be prosperous in the present life, although it was now in the cemetery. A wealthy householder came to the spot and took away the child in the presence of the Master. After the death of the householder, he became the sole master of the household and used to perform meritorious deeds such as acts of charity.

33. *Bhūsapeta*

In a village near *Sāvatthī*, a merchant used to carry on his trade by cheating people with false weights, etc. He increased the weight of the red rice he sold by mixing up red earth with it. His son, again, was no less a sinner; he struck his mother with a whip, saying that she had not shown proper regard for his friends who came to the house. The son's wife ate up the meat kept for other members of the house. When asked about the meat, she flatly denied that she had taken it and swore that if she had eaten it, she would be devouring the flesh on her back from birth to birth. The merchant's wife, also, when anybody asked for anything from her, refused to give it, on the plea that it was not her house, and swore that if she had told a lie, she would eat dirt and excreta from birth to birth. The merchant, his wife, son, and daughter-in-law, were reborn after death as *petas* and *petīs* in the *Vindhya* forest. The merchant as *peta* suffered much from burning chaff on his head and his son used to strike his head with iron clubs. The son's wife, on account of her misdeeds, used to tear pieces of flesh from her back with her big and sharp-pointed nails and eat them up, and thus suffered endless misery. The merchant's wife prepared sweet-smelling and excellent *sāli* rice as her food, but as soon as it was touched by her, it turned into dirty excreta full of vermin and stench and she had to eat it with both her hands. Once the venerable *Mahāmoggallāna* saw them thus suffering and asked them the reason. The merchant's wife told him the past history of all of them as described above and now asserted that inevitable was the consequence of every deed.

34. *Rathakārīpeta*

In the time of *Kassapa Buddha*, a woman who was very pious, used to perform many meritorious deeds. She built a beautiful house for the *Bhikkhu-Saṅgha* (the congregation of the faithful) and Buddha together with the *Bhikkhus* was invited there. After feeding them there, she offered the house to the *Saṅgha*. She was reborn as a *Vimāna-petī* near *Rathakāra* lake in the Himalaya on account of some of her misdeeds. As a result of the merit acquired by offering a house to the *Saṅgha* in her past life, the *petī* got a splendid palace with a very nice tank and beautiful garden. Her complexion was that of gold and she was exquisitely beautiful. She lived there in the midst of celestial splendour, but her long nights passed without the company of the other sex. Thinking of some means to get a mate, she threw into the river a good ripe mango, hoping that the man who would pick it up, might feel inclined to seek for its source. The other details of the story are the same as those of the story described below.

35. *Kaṇṇamuṇḍapeta*

During the time of *Kassapa Buddha*, in the city of *Kimbila*, there lived a certain *Upāsaka* who had reached the state of *Sotāpatti*, the first grade of sanctification. In the company of five hundred other *Upāsakas* of equal faith, he used to perform many good deeds such as the building of hermitages and bridges and collected wealth for the poor and the needy and they erected a *vihāra* and made it over to the *saṅgha*. From time to time they used to go to the *vihāra*. Their wives also followed them in their good deeds, paid visits to the *vihāra* and rested sometimes in beautiful gardens. Once some wicked persons seeing that the wives of the *Upāsakas* were taking rest in the garden, became enamoured of their beauty; but knowing of their virtues and good conduct, discussed among themselves whether any one of them could lead any of them astray. One of the rogues agreed to do this on condition that his associates would give him 1,000 coins in case he was successful in his attempt but that in the event of his failure he would have to pay the above mentioned sum to them. Thus tempted he composed songs and to the accompaniment of a seven-stringed harp, began to sing in a very sweet voice and thereby attracted the attention of one *Upāsikā* whom he at last succeeded in seducing. He thus won the wager of a thousand coins from his fellows. The other rogues thus losing the money informed the husband of the woman. When her husband asked her whether she was guilty; she flatly denied the charge and took an oath pointing to a dog standing close by, that if she were guilty, a black and earless dog like the one there, might eat up her flesh from birth to birth. The other women also were asked about it but they, though fully aware of the misdeed of the fallen woman, replied that if they had known anything about it, they would become servant girls from birth to birth. The unchaste woman died, tortured with the thoughts of her misdeed, and was reborn as a *vimānapetī* residing on the shore of the *Kaṇṇa-muṇḍa* lake. All round her house there were beautiful gardens with nice tanks, and after death the five hundred women, her associates, were reborn as her maid-servants. The woman used to enjoy happiness during the day but at midnight, she used to go to a tank and a terrible black and earless dog used to bite her and throw her into the tank. As soon as she came out of the tank, she regained her beautiful appearance. Thus she stayed there for a very long time with her five hundred women attendants. All the women, however, became restless, as they had no male companions. They at last came to a river which flowed into the Ganges through a mountain fissure from the *Kaṇṇamuṇḍa* lake. There was a miraculous mango tree near their house and the woman threw some mangoes into the river, hoping that some men would pick up the fruits and come to them. One of the mangoes reached Benares, having been carried down the stream. The king of Benares got it, cut out a slice, gave it to a thief in the prison to taste it. The man reported that it was of extraordinarily sweet taste ; the king then gave him another slice which removed the signs of age from his body and restored his youth. The king ate up the rest of the mango and feeling a change in his body, he sent one of his forest-rangers in search of the mangoes. The man received directions from three ascetics whom he met on the way and came to the spot where the women were, but as he had done no deed which might qualify him to enjoy the pleasure provided at the place, he became terrified and returned to Benares and informed the king of the wonderful things he had seen. The king's curiosity being roused, he at once went out with a forest-guide and reached the spot. The women sported with the king who became very handsome on taking the mango. The king stayed with them for a long time and one midnight saw the *vimānapetī* going to the tank and being bit by a dog as described above. The king killed the dog with an arrow and the woman regained her beautiful appearance after a bath in the tank. Then the king asked her the reason of it and was informed of her past history. The king being disgusted, wanted to go back to his own country, notwithstanding the strongest remonstrance from the *petī*, but she was at last persuaded to convey him to Benares. She left the king with lamentations and wailings and the king moved with emotion, did many acts of charity and acquired great merit.

36. *Abhijjamānapeta*

There was a hunter in a certain village near the Ganges, opposite to Benares. He used to kill deer and after roasting and eating the better part of the flesh, brought the rest to his house, tied up with leaves. When he returned to the village with the venison, the boys seeing meat in his hands used to ask for it and to get small bits. One day, getting no deer to hunt in the forest, he took some *uddālaka* flowers to the village and when, as usual, the boys asked for meat he gave a bunch of flowers to each. The hunter, after death, was reborn as a *peta* naked and fierce in appearance and never saw any food or drink. Dressed with garlands of *uddālaka* flowers, he walked on foot in the river against the current of the Ganges, hoping that he would get something to eat from his relations in his village. At that time, a high officer of King Bimbisāra of Magadha named *Koliya*, after suppressing a rebellion in the frontier provinces, was going down the Ganges in a boat after sending away his army on the land route. He saw the *peta* and asked him, " Where are you going thus dressed ? You are walking on foot in the midst of the Ganges. Where is your dwelling house ? " The *peta* replied, " Oppressed with hunger, I am going to my village near Benares." The high minister stopped his boat, gave to an *Upāsaka* who was a barber some articles of food and a pair of yellow clothes, on behalf of the *peta* who was, as a result of that, clothed and fed. He reached Benares before sunrise. The Blessed One was at that time on the banks of the Ganges and the minister invited him to his house. A fully decorated canopy was prepared for the Buddha who sat under it. The high minister worshipped the Master and spoke to him about the *peta*. The Buddha desired the presence of the *Bhikkhu-saṅgha* and many *bhikkhus* came there. The high minister satisfied the Buddha and the *bhikkhus* with good food and drink. After taking food and drink, the Buddha desired the presence of the inhabitants of the outskirts of Benares and many *petas* were brought to the spot and made visible by his miraculous power. Among the *petas*, some were seen naked, some dressed in torn rags, some were seen hiding their naked body with hair, some were oppressed with hunger and thirst and some were mere bones covered with skin. The horrible condition of the *petas* was seen by the people present there. Under the influence of the Buddha's miraculous power, the *petas* themselves described their former misdeeds and their sufferings resulting therefrom. Thus when the results of good and bad deeds had been unfolded before the people, the Master out of his infinite compassion delivered a long discourse expounding the *dharma* to the people.

37. *Ubbarīpeta*

At *Sāvatthī*, an *Upāsikā* lost her husband and overwhelmed with grief, she went to the cemetery and wept bitterly. The Buddha noticing in her the sign of fruition of the first stage of sanctification, went to her house, feeling pity for her. The *Upāsikā* worshipped him with great devotion and then sat on one side. The Buddha asked her about the cause of her misery and she admitted that she was mourning the loss of her beloved husband. In order to remove her sorrow, the Master related the following story of the past :—

In the kingdom of *Pañcāla*, in the town of *Kapila*, there was a king who went by the name of *Cūḷani Brahmadatta*, who was very pious and impartial. He used to perform ten kinds of kingly duties. One day, in order to see how his subjects were doing and to know how they would speak of him, he assumed the guise of a tailor, went out of town alone and wandered from village to village and from province to province. Finding his whole kingdom free from troubles and diseases and the subjects living in safety and happiness, he set out for his capital. While returning, he went to the house of a poor and distressed widow in one of the villages, who inquired of his whereabouts. He introduced himself as a tailor working for wages, and said, " If you have any cloth to be sewn and agree to give me food and wages, I shall show you my skill." She had no work for him. After staying there for a short time, he saw that her daughter was very handsome and had all the auspicious signs. Learning that the girl was yet unmarried, he sought her hand, and with the permission of the mother, married the damsel and lived there for a few days. Then the king in the guise of a tailor, gave them a thousand *kahāpaṇas* and asked them not to be anxious, as he would soon return. Shortly afterwards, the king brought the daughter of the widow to the palace with great pomp and splendour and made her his chief queen, giving her the name of *Ubbarī*. They lived in great conjugal felicity for a long time. The king died and the queen was overwhelmed with grief. The funeral ceremony of the king was performed with great pomp. The Queen *Ubbarī*, however, was inconsolable. She went to the burning-ground and for many days offered flowers and perfumes to her deceased husband, recited his many virtues and went round the cemetery, crying and weeping bitterly like one gone mad.

At that time, the Master, who was then a *Bodhisatta,* resided in a forest near the Himalayas and saw her thus plunged in sorrow, and coming to the cemetery, inquired why she was weeping and crying, taking the name of *Brahmadatta* and he was told that it was for the deceased King *Brahmadatta* that his Queen *Ubbarī* was crying. Moved by compassion, the *Bodhisatta*, in order to remove her sorrow, addressed her thus : " Knowest thou that eighty-six thousand persons bearing the name of *Brahmadatta* were burnt here. Which of them are you lamenting for ? " She replied that she was mourning for her husband, the King of *Pañcāla*, named *Cūḷaniputta*. The *Bodhisatta* assured her thus : " All the *Brahmadattas*, burnt here were of the same name and designation and had been kings of *Pañcāla* and thou hadst been the Chief Queen of them all. Why art thou lamenting for the latest *Brahmadatta* leaving the earlier ones ? " Thus by a discourse on *kamma* and on the many births and deaths that beings have to go through in this world and also by expounding to her the *dhamma*, he consoled her lacerated soul. The queen realized the worthlessness of the household life and receiving ordination from the *Bodhisatta*, embraced the homeless condition and wandered from village to village until she reached *Uruvelā* where she laid down her life and reached the *Brahmaloka*. The *Upāsikā* got rid of her grief, listening to this discourse of the Master who also expounded to her the four great truths.

38. *Suttapeta*

Long before the appearance of the Buddha, near *Sāvatthī*, there was a *Paccekabuddha*, and a boy used to attend upon him. When the boy grew up, his mother brought a beautiful girl for him from a family of equal rank and position. On the day of marriage, when the boy went to bathe with his associates, he was bitten by a snake and died. Although he had accumulated much merit by serving the *Paccekabuddha*, yet he was reborn as a *vimānapeta* on account of his attachment to that girl. But the *peta* possessed great wealth and power and thought of some means of bringing the girl to his abode. If the girl could be made to offer something to the *Paccekabuddha*, his mission would be fulfilled. The *peta* went to the *Paccekabuddha* and seeing that he was in need of some thread to mend his garment, he assumed the guise of a human being, and requested him to go to the girl for thread, if he was in need of it. When the *Paccekabuddha* came to her abode, the girl learning that he wanted some thread, offered him a reel. Then the *peta* bestowed enormous wealth on the mother of the girl and after residing in her house for some time, brought her to his abode. After the Buddha had appeared on the earth, the girl was anxious to come down to the human world to perform righteous deeds and accumulate more merit. The *peta* replied, " You have been here for seven hundred years, if you now go to the human world, you will be very old, all your relatives are dead and gone." Saying this, the *peta* brought the girl to the human world. Old and decrepit that she was, she on reaching her village, did many acts of charity and after seven days she passed away from this world and was reborn in the *Tāvatiṁsa* heaven.

39. *Uttaramātupeta*

After the passing away of the Master and when the first great Council was over, *Mahākaccāyana* lived near *Kosambī* in an *araṇya vihāra* with twelve *bhikkhus*. At this time, an officer of King *Udena*, who was in charge of the construction of buildings, died. After his death, his son named *Uttara* was offered the same post which he accepted. Once *Uttara* desired to repair the city and went to a forest with carpenters to cut down trees for timber. There he saw *Mahākaccāyana* and being pleased with him, approached him to listen to his teachings. He took shelter in the three refuges and invited *Mahākaccāyana* with the *bhikkhus* to his house. He made offerings to the *Thera* and the *bhikkhus* and requested them to take food every day at his house. He also induced his relatives to follow him in this act and built a *vihāra*. But his mother who was stingy and a believer in false doctrines, cursed him by saying, "Let all these offerings which you are making to the ascetics against my wish, be turned into blood in the next world." She, however, approved the act of offering a fan of peacock-feathers on the day of a great ceremony at the *vihāra*. After death, the mother became a *petī*. In consequence of her approval of the fan of peacock-feathers, her hair was blue, smooth, fine and long, and in consequence of her misdeeds, whenever she went down to drink the water of the Ganges, it was at once turned into blood. She suffered for fifty-five years and finding at last a *Thera* named *Kaṅkhārevata* seated on the banks of the Ganges at daytime, she prayed to him for some drink and explained to him her past misdeeds and present wretched plight. Moved by pity, the *Thera Revata* offered drink to the *Bhikkhusaṁgha*, fed them and gave them clothes for salvation of the *petī* and she was soon relieved of her distress.

40. *Saṁsāramocakapeta*

In the past, many heretics of the *Saṁsāramocaka* caste used to live in two villages of *Magadha*. A woman born in a family of the *Saṁsāramocaka* caste in the village of *Iṭṭhakāvati* in *Magadha* used to kill many insects and flies. As a result of her sin, she was reborn as a *petī* who suffered much for five hundred years. In the time of the *Buddha Gautama*, she was born again in another family of the *Saṁsāramocaka* caste in the same village. When she was eight years old, she went to play with other girls in the street. At that time, the venerable *Sāriputta* accompanied by some *bhikkhus*, was going to beg alms along that street. All the girls except the *Saṁsāramocaka* girl referred to above, saluted the *Thera* and the *bhikkhus*. The latter knew that the irreverent girl was a false believer, had suffered much in previous births, and would also suffer in hell in future. He took pity on her and thinking that if she saluted the *bhikkhus*, she would not get into hell but would become a *petī* and would have some chance of salvation hereafter, said to the other girls, " You are saluting me but she is standing stock-still." The other girls forcibly made her salute the *Thera*. Afterwards, she was given in marriage to a young man of another *Saṁsāramocaka* family and when she was with child, she died and was reborn as a *petī*, naked, ugly in appearance, moving about impelled by hunger and thirst. Once the *petī* appeared before *Sāriputta* with a fearful look. The *Thera* inquired of her former misdeeds and the *petī* informed him that she had nobody in her family to be induced to perform meritorious deeds for her and to offer alms to *Samaṇas* and *Brāhmaṇas* on her behalf. She then related her past history and prayed to him for her salvation. The *Thera* gave in charity food, drink, and a bit of cloth to other *bhikkhus* for her sake and in consequence of this, she was freed from the *petaloka* and became as *devatā*. Once she appeared before *Sāriputta* in her celestial grandeur. She was asked how she had acquired it and she said that in consequence of his offering food and drink on her behalf, she got all those celestial things. She further told him that in consequence of his offering that small piece of cloth, she was getting plenty of garments, garments more plentiful than all those that *Nandarājā* got by his conquests. She added that she was happy and had come to salute him.

41. *Sāriputtatherassa Mātupetī*

This *petī* was *Sāriputta's* mother in the fifth birth before the last one when he met the Buddha. Once *Mahāmoggallāna*, *Sāriputta* and others used to live in an *araṇya vihāra*, near *Rājagaha*. At that time, there lived a very wealthy Brahmin at Benares, who used to make unstinted and plentiful offerings to the *Samaṇas* and *Brāhmaṇas* and to the poor and the needy and treated them with all respect and honour. Once he had to go to another place, and before leaving Benares he admonished his wife to continue in his absence all acts of charity just in the same way as he did himself. His wife readily consented to do so. But as soon as he turned his back on Benares, his wife stopped giving offering to the *bhikkhus* and when travellers came to seek for habitation, she pointed out to them a broken and dilapidated house and if any such person came there for food and drink, she abused them, saying, "Eat dirt and excreta, drink urine and blood and so on."

In consequence of her misdeeds, she became a *petī* after death, and had to suffer miseries in consequence of her harsh words. She remembered that she had some connection with *Sāriputta* in her previous birth. Thinking that she might get some relief with *Sāriputta's* help, she went to the gate of the monastery in the forest but was not allowed to enter the establishment. It was only when she introduced herself as the mother of *Sāriputta* in a previous birth that she was allowed to get into the *vihāra*. She appeared before *Sāriputta* and related to him her suffering in the following words: "I was your mother in the fifth birth from the present, now I have become a *petī*. When I am hungry and thirsty, I eat and drink many dirty things. My son, give something in charity on my behalf and relieve me of my sufferings." *Sāriputta* accompanied by *Moggallāna* and others, went to King *Bimbisāra* for alms. The king inquired of their mission and *Moggallāna* intimated to him the objects of their visit. The king sent for his minister and asked him to build four hermitages in a shady forest with good water to drink, and also four *vihāras* with three rooms in each. These were fully furnished and there was abundance of food, drink, clothes, etc., in them. The king offered them to *Sāriputta*, and the latter offered them in favour of the *petī* to the *Bhikkhusaṁgha* headed by the Buddha. The *petī* approved of this charity and was reborn in the *Devaloka*. She afterwards made her appearance before *Mahāmoggallāna* and showed him what a great change her son's gifts had brought about as regards her comfort and happiness.

42. *Mattāpeti*

At *Sāvatthī*, there was a householder who had faith in the Buddha, but his wife named *Mattā*. who was barren, had no faith in the Master and the *Saṁgha*. The householder married another girl, named *Tissā*, lest his family-line should be extinct. *Tissā* had great faith in the Buddha and became the favourite of her husband. She bore a son named *Bhūta*. Being the mistress of the household, she used to make offerings to four *bhikkhus* daily. The barren wife was jealous of her. One day, while both of them were standing together after a bath, the husband, being fond of *Tissā*, began to talk with her, and *Mattā*, out of jealousy, heaped together the sweepings and threw them on the head of her rival. After death, the wicked woman was reborn as a *Petī* who suffered in many ways as a result of her misdeeds. One day, when *Tissā* was bathing in the back part of her house, the *petī* appeared before her and introduced herself to *Tissā* as her former rival in the affection of the householder and related to her how she suffered for her past misdeeds. *Tissā* asked *Mattā* why she had so many impurities on her head and *Mattā* replied that this was the punishment due to her having thrown impurities on the head of *Tissā* in her previous life. *Tissā* further asked *Mattā* why she was scratching the whole body with a piece of the shrub *Kacchu*. *Mattā* replied that once both of them went to bring medicines from the forest ; she added, " You brought medicines and I brought *Kapikacchu* which I spread over your bed. It is for this reason I have now to suffer, as you see." Being further asked why she was nude, *Mattā* replied that once *Tissā* was invited to a relative's house, she went there with her husband and in her absence she (*Mattā*) stole her cloth and it was for this reason she was walking naked. *Tissā* asked *Mattā* why from her body emitted such an intolerable smell and she replied, "Your garlands, perfumes, unguents, etc., were thrown by me into the dung heap and you see the result." *Mattā* added that as she had acquired no merit by any act of charity, she was so much distressed. *Tissā* said that when her husband would return home, she would request him to offer her (*Mattā*) something. The *petī* requested *Tissā* not to bring her husband in her presence, as she was naked. *Tissā* asked what she could do for her. The *petī* requested *Tissā* to invite eight *bhikkhus* and offer them food, etc., on her account. This *Tissā* did and *Mattā* was released from the *petaloka* and after her release she appeared before *Tissā* in splendid attire and showed her what a miracle her gifts had worked and left her with a blessing.

43. *Nandāpeta*

In a certain village near *Sāvatthī*, there lived a householder named *Nandasena*. His wife was *Nandā* who had no faith in the Buddha. She was very stingy and hot-tempered and used to abuse her husband, father-in-law, and mother-in-law. After death, she was reborn as a *petī* near that village. One day, while her husband was coming out of the village, she appeared before him. Her husband asked her the cause of her being a *petī*. She gave him an account of her past misdeeds. The husband said, "Take this upper garment of mine and, clothing yourself with it, come to my house where you will get food and drink and clothes, and you will behold your own dear son." She replied that she was unable to receive anything directly from his hands; if she made gifts for her sake to the *bhikkhus*, then she would profit by it. He did so and she was released from her miseries.

44. *Dhanapālapeta*

Before the appearance of the Buddha, there lived in the town of *Erakaccha* in the country of *Dasaṇṇa*, a merchant who was miserly and a sceptic, having no faith in the Buddha. After death, he was reborn as a *peta* residing in a desert region. He was ugly, rough and fierce, tall as a palm tree. For fifty-five years, he could get neither a drop of water to drink nor a particle of grain to eat. Driven by hunger and thirst, he had to run from place to place. Some merchants of *Sāvatthī* went to the northern regions (*Uttarāpatha*), taking with them five hundred cart-loads of merchandise. While returning, they stopped their carts in the evening under a tree and resolved to spend the night there. The *peta* came to the same spot, parched with thirst; and unable to get water to drink, began to cry bitterly and fell down on the ground like a palm tree uprooted by storm. Seeing him, the merchants inquired about his miserable condition. He answered, "I was a merchant called *Dhanapāla*. Of gold I had eighty cart-loads and of other precious minerals, stones and pearls, I possessed an immense quantity. A master of even this immense treasure that I was, I liked not to spend anything on charity. I ate my food with closed doors and drove away everyone who begged anything of me, with harsh and abusive words. Even when I saw men making gifts, I forbade them. As a result of these and similar other misdeeds, I have accumulated sins without measure, while of meritorious deeds I have none standing to my account. Now all my deeds have brought me to this stage of misery and wretchedness." The merchants moved with compassion for the *peta*, tried to pour water into his mouth but the water could not get beyond his throat on account of his sins. The merchants made inquiries as to the means of releasing him and he told them that if they could make offerings on his account to the Buddha or his disciples, then he would be freed from the *petaloka*. They did so and he was saved from suffering.

45. *Cūḷaseṭṭhipeta*

There was a householder in Benares who had no faith in the Buddha and was very stingy. He did not like to perform good and virtuous deeds. After death, he was reborn as a *peta* whose body was without flesh and blood, and was a mere skeleton. His head was hairless and he was naked. The *peta's* daughter named *Anulā* was in her husband's house at *Andhakavinda* and she desired to feed Brahmins for the sake of her father. The *peta* coming to know of it wished to go to his daughter, went through the sky and reached *Rājagaha*. At that time, *Ajātaśatru*, being instigated by *Devadatta*, killed his father. But he soon repented and, dreaming a horrible dream, he woke up from sleep during the night and, going up to the terrace of the palace, saw the *peta*. He asked the latter, "where are you going, lean and thin, naked creature? You seem to be a monk. Tell me what do you want? I shall try, so far as I can, to fulfil your desire." The *peta* related his past history and intimated to the king that he was going to his daughter who was going to feed *Brāhmaṇas* and make gifts on behalf of himself and the forefathers. *Ajātaśatru* asked the *peta* to go to his daughter and see him on his way back. The *peta* went to his daughter and, when going back, saw *Ajātaśatru*. He informed him that the *Brahmins* to whom gifts were made were unworthy of them, and requested the king to make offerings on his account to the Buddha and his disciples. This was done and the *peta* was relieved of his suffering and by virtue of the merit accruing therefrom, he became a very powerful *Yakkha*.

46. *Revatīpeta*

At Benares lived a householder named *Nandiya* who had faith in the Buddha and was very charitable. Offerings were made to the congregation of monks daily in his house. From his boyhood, he was in the habit of making offerings with his own hands. When he grew up, his parents asked him to marry *Revatī*, the daughter of another householder who used to live near his house. He refused to do so on the ground that *Revatī* had no faith in the Buddha and was uncharitable. The parents of *Revatī* asked her to give some evidence of her faith in the Buddha and of her charitable nature just to win over *Nandiya*. She did so for some time and *Nandiya* married her. She followed *Nandiya* in his meritorious deeds. After some time, *Nandiya* went abroad, asking his wife to continue all the meritorious deeds. After her husband's departure, *Revatī* performed the meritorious deeds for some days. She then not only stopped giving offerings but went so far as to abuse the *bhikkhus* who had come for alms and insulted them. Afterwards *Nandiya* returned home and found that all his acts of charity had been discontinued. After death, *Revatī* became a *petī* and *Nandiya* a *devatā* residing in heaven. *Nandiya* saw with his divine eyes that *Revatī* had become a *petī* and he went to her and reminded her of the consequences of her sinful acts done in the previous existence. He then asked her to approve of the meritorious acts done by him. As soon as she did it, she became a *devatā* and resided with *Nandiya* in heaven.

47. *Aṅkurapeta*

Ten sons and a daughter were born to the king of *Uttaramadhurā* and *Aṅkura* was the youngest of them. The ten princes conquered the whole country beginning from their father's capital called *Asitañjana* up to *Dvārāvatī* and divided it among themselves into ten portions. At the time of partition, they forgot *Añjanadevī*, their sister, but afterwards when they saw that they had left no share for her, *Aṅkura* gave away his own portion and said that he would live upon some money contributed by all the brothers. *Aṅkura* not only engaged himself in trade, but made large gift, always. One of his slaves, however, who was his steward, was a greedy fellow. *Aṅkura*, out of kindness, got him married to a girl of good family, but he died when his wife was with child. When the child was born, *Aṅkura* paid him the salary that he used to pay to his father and when the boy grew up, the question arose whether he was a slave or not. *Añjanadevī* argued that since the mother was free, her child also must be free and he was freed from slavery. The boy went to the city of *Bheruva* and marrying a tailor's daughter followed the profession of a tailor. In that city, there lived a very rich and generous merchant named *Asayha* who was very charitable to the *samaṇas*, *brāhmaṇas* and others. The young tailor could not himself practise charity but he used to point out with his right hand the house of *Asayha* to those who did not know it. After death, this posthumous son was reborn as a god living on a banyan tree in a desert. His right hand could give anything he liked. In that city of *Bheruva*, there was a man who prevented the banker *Asayha* from making gifts and who was, moreover, a false believer and miser. After death, he was reborn as a *peta*, not far from the residence of the above *devaputra*. In the meantime, the great banker, *Asayha*, was reborn in the *Tāvatiṁsa* heaven, as a friend of *Sakka*. Once *Aṅkura* and also a *Brāhmaṇa* merchant were passing through a desert, each with five hundred cart-loads of merchandise. Having lost their way, they wandered about here and there for many days in that arid region. All their stock of food, drink, and fodder became exhausted and *Aṅkura* sent servants in all directions to look out for water. The deity of the banyan tree recollecting the good deeds done by *Aṅkura* in his past life, came to help him and requested him to come under the banyan tree. The banyan tree spread its branches far and wide and *Aṅkura* fixed his tent there. The *Yakkha* stretching his right hand, supplied the whole caravan, first of all, with drink and then gave everything that any one of them might desire to have. Now, when all of them were fully fed and pleased, the *Brahmin* thought within himself, " What should I gain by going to *Kamboja* for money ? I shall capture this *Yakkha* somehow or other and, placing him in my carriage, I shall take him to our city and communicate his thoughts to *Aṅkura*." The latter, however, grew indignant at this proposal and told him, " You wish to cut down the branches of the tree that cast shadow over you." The *Brahmin* retorted that he was ready to cut down the tree itself or to uproot it, if that was sufficiently paying. *Aṅkura*, by discoursing upon the evil consequences of such conduct, silenced the *Brahmin*. The deity himself listening to their discussion, told the *Brahmin* that he was a *Yakkha* of great power and that he was not to be offended with impunity even by the gods, and that it would be impossible for the *Brāhmaṇa* to carry out his desire of taking him to his house. *Aṅkura* then asked the deity how he had acquired the power. The latter then related how, by merely pointing out to beggars the house of a great donor, his hands acquired the miraculous power. *Aṅkura* was thoroughly convinced of the virtue of making gifts and promised that on reaching his own city of *Dvārakā* he would be more liberal than ever and practise charity. The *Yakkha* induced him further to stick to his noble resolve of making gifts and promised that he would help him in carrying it out. He would have punished the *Brāhmaṇa* merchant for his iniquity but *Aṅkura* made the *Brāhmaṇa* obtain his pardon by submission. Leaving the *Yakkha*, not far from the spot, *Aṅkura* met a *peta* who ugly in appearance, his face was awry and his fingers were crooked. On being asked, he said that he was in charge of the charities of *Asayha* and that whenever he saw any one ask for anything, he made a face at him and this was the result. The sight of this *peta* convinced *Aṅkura* that a man should make gifts with his own hands, because the man charged with the work might not do it in the right spirit. On reaching *Dvārakā*, he made gifts on a vast scale and sought to remove the wants of every person he met. His *chargé d'affaires*, *Sindhuka*, a man versed in matters of finance, tried to prevent him from making such gifts without restraint, but *Aṅkura* was not to be dissuaded. Then a large number of persons began to live upon his charities and lead idle lives, leaving their own works and the kings could not get revenue. The kings told *Aṅkura* that if things went on like this their treasuries would be soon depleted. *Aṅkura* thereupon went to the southern country (*Dakkhiṇā-*

patha) in the country of *Damiḷa* and there practised charity and at last, when he left the world, he was reborn in the *Tāvatiṁsa* heaven. Now, during the time that *Gotama Buddha* was here, a man named *Indaka* gave only one spoonful of rice to the venerable *Thera Anuruddha*, and by virtue of that single act of merit, he, after death, reached the *Tāvatiṁsa* heaven and was given a very superior position to that of *Aṅkura*. When the Buddha went to the *Tāvatiṁsa* heaven, all the residents there flocked round the Master, *Aṅkura* had his seat twelve *yojanas* farther than *Indaka* and he learnt then that gifts are to be given to proper persons in order that good results may be produced, just as seeds, if sown on fertile soil, produce crops.

CHAPTER VI

Doctrinal Bearings of the Stories

THE *preta* stories suggest many interesting points for consideration. In the first place, it will be observed that there is no idea of spirit-worship manifest anywhere among the stories; nor is there any semblance of ancestor-worship. Though there is no worship of ancestors in the stories, yet they manifest an anxiety, in some cases, for the welfare and happiness of the deceased forefathers. But even that is not the main lesson of the stories. We meet with references here and there to a devout daughter or a son who offers gifts on behalf of her or his parents, and the latter are relieved of their suffering by such action. But this duty of the progeny is nowhere insisted upon. Nor does it appear that it is only the son who can afford such relief, but everyone can do so. The stories are addressed to Buddhist lay devotees, to *upāsakas* and *upāsikās*, exhorting them to perform meritorious deeds, while on earth, in order to save themselves from personal miseries hereafter. The lesson inculcated logically follows from the law of *karma*, which is the central idea of the whole Buddhistic faith. It is pointed out again and again that the result of *karma*, whether good or bad, cannot be obviated—it is a force which must produce its own consequence. This is sought to be impressed upon the minds of followers of the faith.

The person to whom the stories are addressed is not the seeker after *nirvāṇa* by *prajñā*, *dhyāna* and *samādhi*, nor is he the intellectual seeker after eternal verities or fundamental realities, but the ordinary, everyday man, the seeker after good things of the earth, one who eats, drinks, and multiplies here below, and wishes for plenty of similar enjoyments in the life to follow after death. These advocate that charity here upon earth, charity with a sincere heart while alive, is the only means of commanding the objects of pleasure after death. If one gives away plenty of food and drink, while possessed of the earthly corporeal frame, he will be entitled to enjoy them hereafter, and the converse is none the less true. In this respect the needs of the *petas* and the *petīs* of the stories are identical with those of human beings in flesh and blood; they are oppressed with hunger and thirst. Even the passion of love and desire for companions of the other sex does not leave them, and the strangest thing in this connection is that a lover in the spirit form, whether of the male or of the female sex, enjoys fully the company of a comrade of the other sex who is still in the world of the living. In several stories we hear of a damsel whom a spirit had loved in his former life upon earth being spirited away and released after a number of years; and the opposite side is illustrated when we find the king of Benares being enticed into the garden of the five hundred *petīs* who enjoyed his company.

As regards, however, the other worldly comforts, food, drink, and clothing, it is clearly reiterated many times that a *peta* cannot directly take any of them from here, by force or guile, or even when voluntarily offered; a hand to hand interchange of these things between a *peta* and a man is impossible. It is only when the gifts are made to a human being and the merits thereof transferred to the spirit, that these comforts can reach the *peta* and supply his or her needs. This is the fundamental idea in the Buddhist method of removing the disabilities and miseries of the departed spirits, as also in the Hindu form of *śrāddha*. According to the Hindu idea the gifts are to be made to a Brahmin in person or even to a substitute for a *Brāhmaṇa*, and the merit depends upon the number of people fed and clothed on behalf of the spirit. The fruit of the deeds is transferred to the spirit. In the Hindu *śrāddha*, some articles of food and clothing are of course offered directly to the spirit, but they must be given away to a deserving man in order that the desired results may be produced.

As regards the object of charity, the author of the stories is not without some sectarian narrowness. It is the gifts to the *bhikkhus* and the Buddhist *Saṁgha* that are productive of the best merit, and he invariably speaks of gifts made to them only as having the power to alleviate the suffering of the *petas* and *petīs*. In a few rare cases, he speaks of gifts being made to other religieux but these are ordinary gifts made by bounteous men in the course of their usual charities, not charities for the relief of the *peta*. For that purpose the gift has to be made invariably to a *bhikkhu*, or at least an *upāsaka*, buddhist lay devotee. Even as regards ordinary daily charities, though he does not dismiss as entirely unremunerative the gifts to ordinary human beings not of the Buddhist faith, yet he shows us clearly, as in the story of Prince *Aṅkura*, that even gifts without measure of untold wealth to ordinary denizens of the earth can never produce the same effect as the gift of a small thing to a venerable follower of the Buddhistic persuasion.

The external appearance of the *petas* also closely resembles that of human beings ; in rare cases, we are told, a *peta* was of extraordinary height or had some limbs of a particular extra-human form on account of the deeds done here upon earth. But the general frame of the *peta* is an exact replica of the human figure, as his needs are the counterparts of the worldly comforts of man in his gross form.

The character of the *petas* appears generally to have undergone a change for the better in their spirit-life. Their hunger and thirst, their miseries and sufferings, the bitter experiences for past misconduct, seem to have rubbed off their angularities, softened their temper, chastened their mind, and made them realize the truth that charity is the door to enjoyment of comforts in the other world. We hardly find them doing ill to others, they are too much pressed down with the burden of their own sins to think of or to get any opportunity for doing mischief to others. They are suffering rather than malevolent spirits.

There are various grades among the dead. A broad distinction is made between two classes, the *devas* and the *petas*. The *devas* generally have a preponderance of good and meritorious deeds in their favour, though they are tainted, at least in the lower ranks, with some stain of evil which they have got to work out. The highest among them who have made, like *Seṭṭhi Asayha* or Prince *Aṅkura*, gifts, while on earth, on an immense scale, are born in the *Tāvatiṁsa* heaven, but even here there are innumerable grades. Some of the lower grades among the *devas* are the *Rukkhadevas*, the tree-spirits, and the *Bhūmidevas*, the spirits of the earth, perhaps those whose bonds of attachment to the earth have not yet been cut asunder. *Vimānadevas* are also mentioned, that is, *devas* residing in *vimānas* or palaces in the sky. Between these last and the *Vimānapetas*, there is hardly any line of cleavage and, if any, a very thin one. *Vimānapetas* are the more fortunate ones among the *petas*, those who have some good to their account but not unmixed with some evil which subjects them to suffering and torture. Below them is the great mass of *petas* and *petīs* that suffer intolerable miseries; one gets quite sick when reading the shocking and often revolting accounts of the punishments to which they are subjected. The most loathsome things are narrated of them and when the release comes at last, resulting from a simple act of charity in their favour, the contrast is often very great. It remains for us to say something about the place where the fallen spirits suffer. In many cases, it is related, when the offence was very serious, the sinner suffered for thousands of years in hells and then they came up to wear out the remnants of their sin as *petas*. Descriptions of these hells have not been given in any detail, and of the hellish tortures only some vague references have been vouchsafed to us.

From the hells they come up to the upper regions and go through a purgatory, as it were, in their *peta*-life, until some kind human being frees them from it by transferring the merit of some charity to their account. Many of the *petas* are described as having been transformed into the *peta* beings, directly they died, without going into hell.

Such are the ideas of the spirits and of the spirit world in the *peta-vatthu* and its commentary. The stories, though some among them may seem puerile and even absurd, have served to restrain the believer in the words of the great Master from deviating from the path of virtue, in his thought or his word or his deed, and made him practise charity and *ahiṁsā* towards all living creatures.

INDEX